# PRAISE FOR THE ORG

I am so inspired by The Orgasmic Entrepreneur! I felt like I was reading about my own life. OMG it took me on a whole journey.

This book touches on so many relatable topics for me as an entrepreneur. It encourages people to remain true to who we are, especially the parts of us that may seem "weird" or eccentric. This book goes beyond entrepreneurial advice and touches on our overall well-being. It shows how our mental, physical, emotional, and spiritual health all play a part in how we show up in business, in relationships, and in the world. —*Jenny Vaughn*

Melissa has done a stellar job of honing in on something that I've always felt in my heart, but we rarely talk about in the context of success. So much of the marketplace in self-help and business is about mimicking. Yes, it's important and natural to see what worked for others, but that's only half of it. We should be asking what makes us creatively unique and different as well. She does a masterful job of clearly articulating how to step into your vulnerable and pleasurable weirdness to free the enthusiasm that creates luck in business, life and love. Melissa's messages were overwhelmingly therapeutic. Her words and personal experiences, peppered with those of the individuals she collaborated with, were not only timely but so intimately relevant in a way that is truly difficult to put into words. —*Jason Bernardo*

The Orgasmic Entrepreneur is a book that will take you on a delightfully wild rollercoaster ride with the chaos of life...helping you to align your uniqueness in the world with purpose and joy. A must read...even if you aren't an entrepreneur!!! —*Dr. J. Blackmon*

Chapter after chapter, Melissa seemed to referee—and moderate—my less-than-positive self-talk, a voice that has had me frozen for years.

I could not read this book faster than a snail's pace, even though I did try—I was focused on all the nourishment that was being offered.

This compilation of words, this transparent sharing of feelings, this gentle yet powerful push...I honestly cannot explain how this book made me feel. **I had no idea that this book was written for me.** —*Rebecca Lane*

This book is so appropriate and needed. It felt like an active read, the kind you want to bookmark specific pages to come back and reread or make notes in the margin. The way the author seamlessly moves through and interweaves the topics, I found myself stopping a lot to think. It made me very introspective and spurred me to evaluate my business, processes, real goals for life, and what I need to do to live life on my terms. I have a list of things to work on just based on my first reading.

Melissa has a real knack for writing about business, self-growth, personal development, and spirituality. Even though she frequently refers to "woo woo" stuff, it's written so that it feels like she's unearthing natural truths for us. The content is easy to digest and apply.

I also liked that she used contributors from such varying backgrounds, from her son to other successful entrepreneurs. The book incorporates lessons from everywhere, and it all tied in very smoothly and nicely. — *Rouchelle Fountain*

# THE ORGASMIC ENTREPRENEUR

# THE ORGASMIC ENTREPRENEUR

## DISCOVER THE SWEET SPOT OF LOVE, SEX, AND BUSINESS BY SIMPLY BEING YOU

### MELISSA DRAKE

Featured Authors
JESSE PANAMA, JO DECHENNE, STACEY HERRERA, AND MARTA WILDE

Published by Ultimate Vida, LLC.

978-1-7351659-3-6 E-Book (Kindle)
978-1-7351659-8-1 Paperback (P.O.D.)
978-1-7351659-5-0 Hardback

*For the seekers, the dreamers, and the believers*

# CONTENTS

# ACKNOWLEDGMENTS

I'm happy to be standing in this place and time with a completely different reality than the one I claimed and previously expected as my life path. As tough as it was to break the mold to live and work differently than the way I was taught, I ultimately understand the power of choice, the purpose of new paths, and the value of personal rebellion. I'm grateful to the insurance industry for providing me with 25 years of hardcore corporate experience. I'm even more thankful for the job elimination in 2015 that was the kick in the pants I needed to take responsibility for my emotional and physical health, embrace the destiny I was born for, and pursue my dreams. This book is part of the culmination of pursuing a brand-new path.

For me, and I suspect many others, the greatest lessons come from contrast. When we understand what we don't want, it's easier to understand what we *do* want. My parents were incredibly hard-working and showed me what it looks like to work hard and go out of your way to earn respect, admiration, and financial "security" through work. Their lives reflected beliefs that nothing comes easy, all things of value require hard work, and play—and even rest—must be earned. They also indirectly showed me how relying solely on employers can be detrimental to personal health, wellness, and longevity.

When my father had a stroke at age 56 that rendered him unable to work, I saw how crushed he was to literally lose his identity, independence, and sense of self, which was inextricably linked to his work. In addition to reorienting his life as a sudden retiree, he had to relearn everything, including his own name, his family members' names, how to tie his shoes, and how to eat. Rather than getting bitter, he got better —and so did our relationship. He became such a goofy and fun guy who had a new sense of interdependency that enabled him to be open to support from others. In all honestly, he couldn't function without help. His stroke forced him to surrender, which actually worked to his benefit. He learned to accommodate his disability and did his best to get the most from his new life.

My mom became the sole breadwinner after my dad's stroke. When her job was eliminated at the age of 62, she was understandably bitter. Rather than surrender to the opportunity of the new path offered by her layoff, she took the loss personally and fought against it—legally and emotionally. As good as other aspects of her life were, she frequently blamed her employer for "ruining her life." It was no surprise to me that she promptly got very sick and died shortly thereafter.

My parents' trials related to their work-dependence and their lack of personal health and wellness was an eye-opener for me. Their experiences convinced me there's a different path and I became determined to find it. I'm grateful to have been vicariously shown, through them, the things I don't want. Their examples give me the courage to go after my passions with my whole heart.

In the process of pursuing my new path, I studied extensively. To all the authors and teachers who have shared their work via books, courses, and other content, I'm pleased to have learned from you. Your words expanded my world view and lent quotable passages to support the messages in this book. A full list of works I've cited is included in the resource section at the back of this book.

This book came together while collaborating with my friend and client, Jesse Panama. You'll read more about his story later on, but for now, I must recognize him for holding space for my healing, loving me through my triggers, and holding me to my highest possible vision of success.

I'm so grateful for the teachers, healers, and friends who have helped me learn to transform my experiences. I'm especially appreciative of Mayra Aceves. Our chance meeting in a personal development program angled my life into a refreshing and new trajectory.

I'm grateful for each of the featured authors who offered their expertise to add additional perspectives to this book's narrative. Jesse Panama, Jo DeChenne, Stacey Herrera, and Marta Wilde—thank you for signing on to my vision and sharing your heart and story with the world. I love and appreciate you.

In addition to the featured authors, other peers and connections offered their expertise and allowed me to share some of their social media content. Thank you to Beth Derrick, Tiffany Hawthorn, Linda Gordon, and Wendy Burrell for lending your voice to the message of *The Orgasmic Entrepreneur*.

Aside from the tales offered by others, all the stories in the book came from personal experiences and are written from my own vantage point. I offer a huge shout-out to the individuals who helped me see things in a new way, provided new insights, and helped me to learn more about myself on the path to becoming an orgasmic entrepreneur. The coaches, mentors, and contacts mentioned by name in the book gave permission to be named. While not all of the insights included are attributed to a specific person, the inspiration and impact was invaluable and I'm happy to pass it on to impact others as well.

# INTRODUCTION

I'm a big picture thinker who connects the dots in new and unusual ways. In early 2020, I listened to a podcast about data that may have been boring to some, but completely struck me as profound. The content led me to a very seductive correlation between dating and business, specifically the link between achieving sexual satisfaction and attaining strong business results. I honestly couldn't stop thinking about it. Because of this, I was confident that I needed to write about the correlation I'd created in my mind. As time went on, I saw more and more connections between the way entrepreneurs do business and how they "relate" to their larger world. It seems that many of the same principles that apply to intimacy also prevail in the way we work— especially for entrepreneurs. This realization led me to expand writing on the topic from an article to a book in order to address all the connections I discovered.

Over time, the idea and outline for *The Orgasmic Entrepreneur: Discover the Sweet Spot of Love, Sex, and Business by Simply Being YOU* was born. Because I'm not exactly there yet, as in having discovered the "sweet spot," I relied on collaborators to tell the whole story. With the help of some fantastic peers and featured authors, I'll present these connected principles with specific examples from both a business and intimate relationship perspective. The concepts will be eye-opening, provocative, and maybe even a bit mindfucking. Fair warning: This is not a buttoned-up, dry, corporate exploration; there will be swearing, rebellion, and a touch of woo.

I've personally worked with every featured author. Each was chosen for their unique perspective, experience, and authority over the subject matter they're contributing. The result includes diversity in writing style, including notable differences in UK spellings and measurements. Because the primary message is about being your true self and living life on your terms, it was essential for me not to adjust the authors' natural expressions and complete excessive edits on their contributions.

Much of this book's content is non-traditional. That includes open discussions of sexuality, dating concepts, and uncommon ways of doing business. Because I've lived my life as a heterosexual woman and many of the book's stories are personal, most include male and female examples. Regardless, the meanings are universal and applicable regardless of one's gender identification or sexual orientation.

I'm excited to share these concepts with you and I hope you'll stay in touch so we can continue this important and revolutionary discussion. It's my belief that topics like sexuality, wealth, and big ideas, often considered "taboo" are the exact topics that require more dialogue.

*"There is only one success—*
*to be able to spend your life in your own way."*
—CHRISTOPHER MORLEY

# CHAPTER ONE

## AN EXCHANGE OF THE HEART

When my 25-year career in the insurance industry came to an end after an utterly unexpected job elimination, I took it as a blessing—not even in disguise. Just a few months before, during an energy session, I was told, "You have 100% of your heart invested in your job. Are you sure insurance is the place you want to extend **all** of your heart energy?" My reply was blunt and honest, "Fuck no. That's not where I want to invest my heart."

As a single mother from the time my son was two years old, he was my priority and the place I wanted to devote my heart. Outside of my parental responsibility, there was little time or energy to assert in other ways. But work? I was truly dedicated to my employer because that's what my parents demonstrated. Regardless of the ebb and flow of my life over my 25-year career with only three employers, I remained committed to my profession. My commitment was constant while battling severe depression and barely managing to get out of bed. It didn't waver when I attended college full-time as a single parent, nor while dealing with the crushing demands of the sandwich generation. My work didn't suffer when my mother underwent cancer treatments, nor did it falter when I cared for my parents as they died in hospice less than one year apart. My performance remained steadfast when my son left for college and two concurrent chronic illnesses presented on top of empty nest syndrome. No matter what was going on, I always executed at work and received exemplary reviews. Although my job performance and salary were remarkably high, there were undoubtedly many things missing from my work's reciprocity, namely *me* and the ability to truly be me. My work environment didn't allow me to connect with others, share my heart, and be true to my spirit. Corporate life left me feeling stifled, suppressed, and stuffed into a box of its "acceptable" terms, many of which insulted my soul.

Even when it came to my own body, I was not free to express myself in my corporate experience. Freedom of expression is one of my most significant values, only I'd spent most of my life not expressing myself to fit into the box others put around me. In 2017, I threw all caution to the wind and got my first tattoo. It's probably the most meaningful one on my body. It's a semicolon representing suicide survival. A semicolon is used when an author could've ended their sentence, but chose not to; the tattoo serves as a reminder that my story isn't over. This is a humble truth I share with my son and we tattooed its meaning as a constant reminder that we both choose to go on—for ourselves and for one another. My job elimination came shortly after I got my second tattoo memorializing my mother after her death. A few months earlier, one of the consultants close to my CEO boss lectured me about how unsightly tattoos were and advised me not ever to get one—especially considering my role as a director who visits and collaborates with clients and business partners. I often wondered if my new tattoos played a part in why I was let go. Whether or not my body art played a role in my job loss is neither here nor there, but an observation and note about culture. Within days of receiving my elimination notice, I promptly got a new tattoo declaring, "Everything Happens for a Reason." While my new tattoo wasn't inked out of spite, the bold print on my forearm certainly turned a few heads as I worked the final days in my position.

Even though my severance package came with full support to get a new job, including outplacement and job search services, I decided to venture out on my own and find work that was more aligned to the person I'd become. I joined the insurance ranks at the tender age of 19 and had grown up in the industry. By the time I was laid off, I was a 44-year-old single mother recovering from a series of unfortunate experiences, including the death of both parents, two devastating chronic physical illnesses, a host of mental diagnoses, and addictive patterns. I'd also recently discovered social media and Facebook. I immediately immersed myself in learning all I could about healing and taking responsibility to create my own reality. As part of this process, I began connecting with people from all walks of life and was happy to find most of the people I connected with were entrepreneurs.

The thing I've noticed most about entrepreneurs is how unique they are, each having their own brand of solutions to serve their clients. The brands are as numerous as the entrepreneurs, but the rebellious foundation and heart of an entrepreneur is commonly shared. What I surmised was that entrepreneurs are innovators; they are the movers-and-shakers who challenge the status quo. Entrepreneurs are often rebels who are never satisfied with the way things have always been done. Instead, they try new things because they are perpetually striving for more; they are unfazed by economic downturns, difficult political climates, or even global pandemics. Instead, they forge ahead, seeing "problems" as opportunities. Entrepreneurs understand a different approach can lead to different, better results. More importantly, they do what it takes to create new products, services, and outcomes to literally make the world a better place.

The Center for American Entrepreneurship states that "Entrepreneurs play a disproportionate role in commercialization of new products, and essentially all of the most transformative innovations have been brought to the fore by entrepreneurs."[1] Armed with outside-of-the-box strategies, entrepreneurs create new rules, establish new frameworks, and often dominate markets.

There's another thing I've noticed about entrepreneurs. They're often weird or labeled by others as "crazy" because they don't follow traditional rules. And I mean "weird" in the best possible way. In the same way entrepreneurs don't accept the status quo for business results, they also challenge standard mores when it comes to how they look, how they talk, how they value their experience, when, how, and where they work, and the way they interact with people while they work. I've certainly encountered more people with colored hair, tattoos, and piercings in the entrepreneur circles than in the office. And swear words? Fuck! Don't get me started. In my circle of collaborators, the swear words flow with ease. And yes, you'll see several in this book.

Entrepreneurs' experiences differ from the norm as well. Rather than relying on advanced education and stacking degrees, some entrepreneurs use "street cred," like a history of drug dealing, psychedelic journeys, and prison stays as their training ground. For others, their schooling looks more like "personal cred." They see parenting and life's tough transitions like divorce, death, job loss, spiritual awakening, and chronic illness as experiences to help shape their business vision and connect with clients. That's not to say they don't have the education and personal development certifications to back up their credibility, though. It's more like they don't lead with it, or it's simply unnecessary to their work.

Entrepreneurs differ from the norm in their choices of work schedules, creative processes, and location preferences as well. Many prefer to work according to their personal circadian rhythm, no longer tied to a set schedule and an alarm clock. Many often work late nights, insanely early mornings, or in selective spurts throughout the week and weekends. Some, like me, include frequent pauses in their work day for nature walks, dance breaks, field trips to the beach, "psych" breaks (that is, psychedelic intermissions), nooners, or self-pleasure sessions. Yeah, I said it; there's much more of that to come—or should I say to cum?—in the following pages. Entrepreneurs' favored work locations include coffee shops, bars, patios, poolside beach chairs, couches, and beds. Let's not forget that, thanks to technology, work doesn't even have to be "on location" anymore. Recent changes in work, made even more common by the global pandemic, have made the concept of digital nomads, "people who choose to embrace a location-independent, technology-enabled lifestyle that allows them to travel and work remotely, anywhere in the world,"[2] come to life. Some entrepreneurs work from across town, across the country, or across the world, folding international travel into working and meeting with clients. Van life and RV living are other options for business owners and some even choose to cohabitate while working with collaborators. According to MBO Partners, the 2020 global pandemic had a massive impact on the population of digital nomads in the U.S., with an increase of nearly 50% from 2019.[3]

The above variations in work-life balance and execution noted, the one characteristic that's most striking to me about entrepreneurs—at least the ones I work with—is the way they interact with one another while working. First and foremost, they're *real*. While working, entrepreneurs don't hide who they are as people; often, their quirky personal expressions are the cornerstones of their brand. They don't shy away from who they are; they don't suppress their aspirations; and they certainly aren't quiet about their beliefs—even when those beliefs are contrary to the dominant corporate or societal culture. For me, creativity, flexibility, and lack of inhibition are some of the greatest advantages of being an entrepreneur. I can be me all day, every day, whether I'm working, parenting, or enjoying time with a date. I don't have to hide any part of who I am, and I certainly am not accountable to other people trying to put me in a box that limits my abilities. By cultivating my own sense of entrepreneurship and personal development, I've come to better understand my authenticity, vulnerability, sensitivity, and intuitive connection skills; they are the biggest assets to my business success. They are also the exact traits I was asked to eradicate in the corporate world.

The precise traits of authenticity, vulnerability, sensitivity, and intuition also highlight another thing I love about the entrepreneurs I collaborate with. Individual business owners can and do often form intimate connections with their clients, treating them as friends and family members. I've seen them send gifts to one another, spend time connecting personally, and even travel together leisurely. In this realm of united work, it's not uncommon for business partners and collaborators to end client phone calls and Zoom conferences with expressions of love.

Considering all the aforementioned, let's get intimate as entrepreneurs and get this party started!

I'm ready. Are you?


Let's dance!

*"We're all a little weird.*
*And life is a little weird.*
*And when we find someone whose weirdness is compatible*
*with ours, we join up with them and fall into mutually*
*satisfying weirdness–and call it love–true love."*
—ROBERT FULGHAM

# CHAPTER TWO

## HOW TO FIND YOUR PERFECT MATCH

There's no question I'm a little weird. It wasn't until I was in my forties that I began to accept and appreciate the ways I'm different. As I'm nearing the big 5-0, I can say with certainty that the things that make me weird or different are my greatest assets. What does being weird have to do with finding a perfect match?

Absolutely everything.

Actually, it's not so much about being weird as it is about being yourself, and for many of us, especially entrepreneurs, weird comes with the territory. However, as much we appreciate our eclectic characteristics today, most of these characteristics didn't always come with positive reinforcement. Instead, the unique traits were often greeted with bullying and anxious responses, sometimes resulting in codependent patterns to cover eccentric tendencies. Particularly when we're younger and haven't come to accept our quirks as advantageous, it can be instinctual to conform ourselves into who other people want us to be; no matter the amount of personal discomfort we experience.

When I'm forfeiting all of who I am in relationships, whether it's an intimate one, or a professional one, there's bound to be trouble. In my experience, the trouble was all mine. As I bent over backward for other people and repressed my own desires, I internalized all of the angst, and it literally made me sick. I was in a near-constant state of dis-ease. This showed up in severe depression, morbid obesity, chronic illness, and a complete and utter disregard for the yearnings of my heart and soul. You can imagine the result: I lived in a perpetual state of frustration and lack, pleasing other people and not being attentive to my own needs. In other words, I settled...a lot; I settled for a job that didn't light me up, and I settled in relationships that were wrong for me. The result was a massive drain on my life force energy.

Especially in cases with childhood trauma, this reaction to hide our real feelings, personality, and the truth is primarily used as a defense mechanism. In fact, it can even lead to a compulsive pattern of pleasing others and subjugating our own needs. Identified by therapist and author Peter Walker in his book *Complex PTSD: From Surviving to Thriving*, the fawn response is now recognized as the fourth 'f' in the fight/flight/freeze/fawn response to trauma. Here's how Walker describes it: "A fawn response is triggered when a person responds to threat by trying to be pleasing or helpful in order to appease and forestall an attacker." This response is most common in people with anxious attachment and codependency. The pattern of behavior is further represented by Walker as follows: "Fawn types seek safety by merging with the wishes, needs, and demands of others. They act as if they believe that the price of admission to any relationship is the forfeiture of all their needs, rights, preferences, and boundaries."

Ooof. That's a big one. That's the majority of my life summed up in one paragraph. As much as I experienced the personal consequences of fawning, chances are, the people I was in relationships with didn't benefit either. How could they be with the amount of internal strife I was experiencing? As much as I claimed to want to be in that job or relationship and bent over backward to please another, the misalignment was likely felt. Abraham-Hicks, my favorite speaker on the Law of Attraction, explains this phenomenon, noting:

*Often you are pulled this way and that in an attempt to please another, only to discover that no matter how hard you try, you cannot consistently move in any pleasing direction, and so, you not only do not please them, but you also do not please yourself. And because you are being pulled in so many different directions, your path to where you want to be usually gets lost in the process.*

I can confirm this to be true. People-pleasing is a clusterfuck that doesn't please anyone.

When two concurrent chronic illnesses and an empty nest jolted me out of the pattern to put other people's needs ahead of my own, I learned about boundaries for the first time in my life. I was 44 years old. Not surprisingly, this awakening occurred at the same time as my corporate job departure. This blessing allowed me to decide who I was and what I wanted to do with the rest of my career. There was just one significant difference: I decided to search out passionate employment that worked for me and *all* my peculiarities rather than follow expectations. To be clear, it was expected that I'd get another corporate job and continue slogging away, giving my heart to the insurance industry. But I was open and ready for something different. When a co-worker reached out to me after she heard the news I was let go, she was very curious about my next steps. Honestly, I had no fucking clue, but I finally spoke my truth when I answered, "I'm just going to focus on getting well for now. Ultimately, I want to write and help end the stigma of mental illness. I'm also an approved hospice volunteer but have been so sick that I haven't been able to volunteer yet. I'm just going to let God unfold my destiny in the days ahead. It's all good." You know what's cooler? I meant it. It was time to place my heart in something that mattered and really "come out" as the person I was meant to be. I enjoyed working with hospice patients during my severance period. And I was even gifted more personal healing because I worked in the exact center and sometimes even in the same room as where my mom passed five years before.

In terms of my profession, I was coming from a mindset of abundance, trusting the Universe to provide, with the faith that the details of this pivot in my life would line up and the path there would become clearer and clearer. I embraced uncertainty, leaned into curiosity, and pushed forward, following my joy, despite circumstances that, on paper, looked ridiculously bleak. I also fully owned the unique traits I brought to the table; I proudly displayed my tattoos, the number of which multiplied quickly. I wasn't afraid to swear, and most importantly, I revealed my humanness in all my daily interactions with family, friends, and new people I met.

In my coaching and consulting role, I help businesses and individuals find solutions and go further than they thought possible. I'm a Highly Sensitive Person (HSP) and an empath who's full-on "woo." I consider myself a bit of a mystic midwife assisting others to conceive, birth, and grow their creations. I work primarily with stories and do everything from helping people write and publish their articles and books, to establishing their online presence and social media platform, and promoting their stories through an ecosystem that delivers leads and manage the sales process. I believe in many things that aren't main-stream. Because my beliefs are a part of who I am and help me with the work I deliver, I make no attempts to hide them. In fact, there are certain services I purposefully market as intuitive, even though "intu-itive" and "professional" skills appear to be an uncommon match in the same way "intimacy" and "business" are not commonly related. My biggest, most lucrative client approached me about editing services after their project manager chose me specifically because my website mentioned intuitive skills. This uncommon blend of sensitivity and professional expertise creates the strong foundation that makes my services unique. I'm really in tune with other people, and I'm also ridiculously perceptive and heart-centered. I approach business with the same love and attention that I share with my family and friends.

There is an advantage to being clear about who I am and marketing my services; I can better connect with others who have the same values of integrity, professionalism, and a desire to make the world a better place through our work. In many cases, we're already in alignment because we have similar beliefs. Also, when you have a very specific niche, there are often raving fans who are seriously committed to your specific offering. I met a chef at an event who curated cannabis and psychedelic mushroom experiences and meals. As a vegetarian himself, he debated on making his culinary business vegetarian as well. He was concerned about limiting his clientele with this change. However, after making the change that aligned with who he was as a person, his business grew exponentially. That's no coincidence.

Dedicated, raving fans who flock to business owners with a specific and unique offering have the same disposition and heart that I'm looking for in intimate partnerships. I want partners who choose to be with me *because* I'm different, not because I'm the same as everyone else.

*I desire to connect and work with people*
*who accept the most unusual and weird parts of me*
*as readily as they accept*
*the more mainstream ones.*

There's one major advantage to really being who I am in dating and in business: I can be human and authentic at all times. There's no need to compartmentalize different aspects of myself. There's nothing to hide and no need to adjust who I am in the moment or based on the company I'm around. I'm simply unapologetically me—all the time.

My friend Beth Derrick is a little weird like me. In fact, all of my best friends—and clients—are weird. As a lesbian with non-traditional views, Beth has experienced bullying and despair to the point where she began questioning everything about herself, including her sexuality. Beth also has one of the most amazing relationships I've ever witnessed. She and her wife Tosca are the most flawlessly matched pair ever. They are truly unique puzzle pieces perfectly made to fit together. If either of them had tailored their puzzle piece to be more "acceptable" in society's eyes, there's no way they would fit together so exquisitely, nor would they have likely matched in the first place.

I've invited Beth to share the story of how she came to be unapologetically herself and how the fantastic gift of Tosca came into her life when Beth fully embraced who she was. I met Beth five years ago though a coaching program we were both enrolled in. In addition to being one of my best friends, Beth is an amazing coach. One of the things I love most about Beth is her judgment-free approach to relating. Her unique coaching skills include her humble humor, the way she listens, and the sound solutions she provides. Beth doesn't blindly subscribe to conventional wisdom; she's holistic in her approach, and she's wildly practical.

Life isn't always practical, though. And sometimes, when life seems to be falling apart, that's the time life is actually falling together. In Beth's own words, here's how she found the advantage of being herself and welcomed her wife Tosca into her life:

> During the hot and steamy summer of 2017, just months before the statistically impossible happened and my soul collided with Tosca's in real life; I'd fully resolved to remain single forever, or until I found my one true love, whichever came first. I had spent over a decade in serial relationships that taught me more than I could've ever learned in any other school of life. Those relationships were emotionally, physically, mentally, spiritually, and financially draining. The plethora of lessons to unpack from those harrowing, forgettable-yet-memorable experiences are near infinite and invaluable, but that's a conversation for another day. We don't have that kind of space and time here.

> "It seems like we're both on dating sites, so I think it's best we call it and end our relationship." That's the summary of a text received in the wee hours as I pulled into Whole Foods for my morning coffee. Spoiler alert: the partner I dated before Tosca signed up for a dating app and found one of my very old profiles on it. I'd

*forgotten about it altogether until that day's reminder. While the relationship had been obviously over months prior, I let her take the lead in officially ending it, so it was on her terms and not a detrimental surprise to me. I was free again, light as a feather, and unchained. Hallefuckinglujah! My feet must have flown me into that Whole Foods coffee bar that morning, because life was good again! The common feelings and experience of breakups are sadness, loneliness, heartbreak, disappointment, letdown, anger, mistrust, pain, relief, confusion, grief, loss, paralysis, purposelessness, and isolation. My feelings were everything opposite of those common ones that day.*

*When that final gift of singlehood was given, I jumped into it with open arms and a grateful, happy, healing heart. By that point, all of the characteristics I desired in my perfect match were muddied by years of mismatched relationships and forced commitments. Most of those encounters shouldn't have gone beyond a second date. For reasons now largely forgotten or unknown to me, I can't articulate why I chose to explore relationships with most partners. I am beyond thankful to each of them for their time, energy, companionship, and lessons. But don't mistake me there; I would not repeat them ever again. This time, being single and the odd wheel to all of my friends' couple hood was suddenly exciting and freeing, whereas it previously felt quite sad and oppressive.*

*I began the next chapter of my life with a very long list of specific characteristics of the type of partner I did not want. Some lovely friends and I stood on the beach in Malibu, California, with our feet in the water just where the salty waves gently lapped against the sand. We stood in those healing waves and talked about life, writing, relationships, and dreaming. One constant was evident to us all: Nothing can stop the waves, but we can control where we stand in relation to them. In the span of those moments, I resolved to stop looking and to no longer put myself in the dangerous depths of the turbulence of unhealthy relationships. My ultimate goal in life has always been to find my person, marry her, and live happily ever after. The actions being taken were not proving fruitful nor directly progressive in that goal, so the variables had to change. That, I did know. What I didn't know was I was not going back, and I was finished compromising and settling for shituations. (Shituations = shitty situations. You're welcome for this new word.)*

*The next few months were spent deeply and uncomfortably questioning everything I knew about myself. Was I a lesbian? Was asexuality a better lifestyle choice? Was I meant to be in a relationship, or was I meant to be single forever? How did I keep going down the wrong relationship paths, thinking the outcome would be any different than the previous? Was monogamy for me? Or was the taboo world of polyamory a better option? Was I wanting too much from one person? Would a Friends With Benefits (FWB) scenario be a better and happier arrangement? Were all of those experiences, signs, and roadblocks, directing me to another path in life altogether, like writing rap songs and making it big? Or focusing on real estate investing and building an empire out of that? The answers to all of these questions were, have always been, and forever will be, clear to who I am at my very core being. Asking them still felt required to explore the possibilities that could have been missed out on. I'd been living narrowly in some regards, so I opened my net wider, so to speak, out of curiosity and the need to bring into my life something that was quite possibly glaringly yet obviously missing from it. This wasn't a solo quest, like most things had been for me, it was one where I actively engaged in conversations with friends so I could garner their life experiences and perspectives. It was an exploratory, enlightening, and confirming exercise. It was also necessary to ask uncomfortable and somewhat preposterous questions of myself; otherwise, the unknown might have perplexed me indefinitely.*

*My life was calling for me to engage in all manner of practices that resonated healing and formulated a plan for a healthier and happier existence. Knowing myself well enough to know that I need to dig in and do the damn work to learn anything, led me to a heap of writing exercises, exploring my fears, dreams, wants, and needs. It also taught me to communicate effectively, especially when the words are uncomfortable. As a formally passive-aggressive communicator, this was beyond intimidating, and very nearly debilitating. But, it was doable, and I was determined to be self-aware enough to be coachable and growable.*

*Whatever my life evolved into was going to be my decision, and mine alone. I was so completely over trying to make other people happy, on any level. A certain thriving force of selfishness must exist in order for us to serve others in an honest and authentic manner. This was like the final piece of the equation to unlock the door to get to my person. The more I am myself, the better I can be of service to her, our family, the entire world at large.*

*I knew she was out there. I looked everywhere, every single day, in every imaginable place. From Dallas to Singapore, my eyes were wide open, looking for her beautifully perfect face and her big, curly hair. Each time I saw someone that reminded me of this magical person I hadn't yet met in this life, I made eye contact or struck up a conversation, only to learn that my search remained in full force. The funny thing is, Tosca worked in an office building I drove by hundreds of times. We were so close, yet so far away.*

*The loneliest I'd ever felt as a human was in the presence of others. Many feel lonely when they're alone, but before I met Tosca, that's when I felt the most alive. The feeling in relationships before Tosca was like eating a peanut butter sandwich, when you really wanted to have a filet mignon smothered in garlic butter. Sure, peanut butter sandwiches satiate the hunger craving, but not with the immense satisfaction of a perfect steak. I force-grew myself out of peanut butter sandwiches. I wanted the filet mignon!*

*My very unhealthy pattern of dating people, hoping they'd turn into someone they weren't, was too prevalent for too long. I settled and it sucked. People are who they are, and the willingness to be in a relationship with another person is only a very small component of the larger algorithm of happiness, love, commitment, compatibility, and longevity.*

*Do you know that bubbling of energy in a pot of water right before it boils? That's exactly what the weeks leading up to my first encounter with Tosca felt like. I buzzed with anxious anticipation, knowing that something was about to happen, but I didn't know what, when, or how. Every day felt like a race from wake to sleep, diving through the depths of anxious energy, with no reason I could identify as justification. The boiling, in this case, was our first exchange of messages on a dating app. And the rest, as they say, is history.*

*When Tosca and I met, my heart was instantly and permanently full, elated, grounded, excited, known, and free. Everything began to make sense, in all of life's non-mental capacities. I could breathe and relax for the first time—possibly ever, knowing I'd found my one true love. The things in me that were once picked apart by others are celebrated by this beautiful soul named Tosca; the characteristics that were previously ignored are appreciated by her.*

There's no question Beth and Tosca are a perfect match. As Beth's story demonstrates, the key components contributing to finding her perfect match are putting oneself first, being totally honest, and showing up as completely and totally authentic, no matter how weird. In other words, Beth searched within to find her best self and showed up unapologetically. In return, she is wholly and completely loved, appreciated, and admired. I can think of no better reason to be authentic.

*"Love yourself enough to set boundaries.
Your time and energy are precious.
You get to choose how you use it.
You teach people how to treat you by deciding what
you will and won't accept."*
—Anna Taylor

# CHAPTER THREE

## CULTIVATING AN ABUNDANT MINDSET

Entrepreneurs charge a premium for their time and services. They don't accept all the clients who want to work with them and they certainly don't reply to all the direct messages they receive on social media. Before choosing to do business with each other, they often schedule a discovery meeting to ensure their offer is a match to the prospect's needs, they're a good fit for the service, the client is willing to do the work, and can pay for the products and services they desire.

Successful and seasoned entrepreneurs don't take every opportunity that comes their way. Most won't settle for a job or a client that's not a match or doesn't pay well. Instead, they hold out for a more aligned opportunity, which is easier said than done. Most people are trained in the matrix of lack where it's better to have something rather than nothing. As a result, they settle, clinging to crappy people, misaligned jobs, and low-paying clients. Commanding alignment when it comes to pulling in new business requires an abundance mindset and having trust in the value provided. An abundance mindset leads with the understanding that there's more than enough business for everyone, that it's worth sticking to a viable offer, and that getting it in front of the right people at the right time is super important. It's knowing that releasing or saying "No" to less-than-ideal clients leaves room for more and greater opportunities to arrive.

In 2020, a website I applied to write for notified me they would not be moving forward with a contract. They invited me to stay in touch if I gained some experience and published bylines. My knee-jerk and scarcity-based response was, "You mean 30 years' experience and more than 100 bylines with 14 different publishers isn't enough? How can I make this work? What do I need to do to prove I can do this?"

In the past, when I'd get rejected (in business or in love), my tendency was to adjust my approach and sometimes *myself* to please other people and garner their acceptance. My own health and evolution suffered as a result of this pattern. It is also clearly based in a lack mentality of not owning my value and attempting to grasp and retain things that aren't a good fit. Instead, it's healthier to trust the Universe is leading me to my desires. Trust begins with the faith that I'm deserving and poised to receive what I wish.

After taking a breath and centering myself when I lost the website writing contract, my self-aware response was an abundant one. I thought to myself, "Oh, I guess this means something bigger is in the works. I'll trust this redirection and hold out for something that's more aligned. Everything is happening perfectly." Not 30 minutes later, I received a PayPal notification with payment for a job that offered 10 times the revenue, working with a client who I deeply admire and respect.

I experienced the most growth in my business when I became more discerning and said "No" to potential clients. This was particularly true when I said "No" from a place of worthiness and abundance. A few years ago, I coached a client in doubling the price of their offer. With every inquiry that came in, my client and I stood firm in the value of the offer. We believed wholeheartedly in the product offering and oper-ated from an unshakable certainty that there was a plethora of people to contract with. This move elevated the clientele we worked with, brought in more revenue, and eliminated the pattern of operating in a valley of doubt, self-consciously lowering prices and taking on every person who wanted to pay a few bucks for our services.

Recently, I encountered a copywriter, Tiffany Hathorn in a Facebook group for freelance copywriters. When a person posted her worries about losing a client due to a price increase and was unsure what to do, Tiffany chimed in with this response that perfectly demonstrates what it's like to own—and benefit from—an abundance mindset:

> *You didn't lose the client because you asked for too much money. They went with someone else because their budget can't accommodate the rate you decided is fair for you and they found someone who is willing to do the project for cheaper. Period.*
>
> *I'd honestly rather have a reputation for charging a rate that maybe not everyone can afford than to be known as a cheap option. Trust me, I've learned from experience that being the "cheap and great" option fricking SUCKS because you end up with a ton of paid work yet still struggle to make ends meet, which is one of the prime recipes for burnout.*
>
> *I personally wouldn't go back to them with anything other than well-wishes (and maybe not even that if it's been more than a day or two since they made that decision). If you've already responded in any form since they let you know, I wouldn't bother at all. They've moved on and now you can too—to better-paying projects.*
>
> *As an analogy, imagine someone ended a relationship with you because you told them about a new set of standards you set for yourself and they thought you expected too much. Would you go back to them and say "If you take me back, I'll lower my standards for you?" Or would you try to make your peace with the relationship being over (even if it's hard) and be open to a relationship that's exactly what you want?*

*P.S. I wouldn't burn the bridge. I just wouldn't reach back out to offer any lower prices. Your prices are what they are now. If they want to work with you in the future, it should be based on your new rates. I've definitely had clients who couldn't afford to work with me after I raised my rates and actually REFUSED to pay me less when I offered to grandfather them in (because I'm a recovering people-pleaser, lol). They said they'd just come back when they could afford to pay what I asked for. And they did. So it hurt in the short-term to "lose" them, but in the long-term, it was better.*

Having an abundance mindset isn't just appropriate for the business world, it applies to dating as well. Just like business owners whose products and services are high-value, a certain subset of the dating pool is, too. In reality, every single person is high-value because they exist. However, not everyone shows up in the dating world representing the inherent value they possess. Nor do they match what I'm looking for in a romantic partner. Like beauty, value is in the eye of the beholder, and is very subjective. Here's what a high-value dater and good match looks like to me: They love themselves and take their life, passions, and purpose seriously. They recognize and own their worth; they have plans and aspirations for their career and they're getting after it. While imperfect, they have their shit together and take care of their business; they pay their bills on time, they have a place to live, they have transportation, and they consistently show up for themselves. They also show up for the people they care about, but are careful not to give away their power or lose their own connection. They take care of their home and their mental, physical, spiritual, financial, and emotional health; they're creative and express themselves clearly—impeccable grammar and a robust vocabulary is a huge plus! While they may work hard, they also understand the importance of play and make rest and recreation a priority. They're honest and transparent about their needs; they're respectful, considerate, and mature; they are self-aware and continually develop their personal and professional skills; they are emotionally-available and working to resolve traumas and other issues that contribute to a less-than-optimal life. They have friendships and other relationships that are meaningful and add reciprocal value to their lives.

Like successful entrepreneurs, high-value daters don't easily give away their time, and they don't respond to breadcrumbs. Now, I haven't done this perfectly, but when a man, especially one I've just met, sends me a low-effort text inquiry "wyd" text, asking, "What are you doing?" I'm not likely to respond. In fact, I may even block him—especially if it arrives after 10 pm with the energy of a player expecting a booty call. "Wanna hang out?" Nope. No thank you. "Hanging out" is the equivalent of Netflix and Chill and is something I do with people I know and love, not strangers who want to hook up. If a man is truly interested in me, and by me—I mean who I am as a person—my mind and my heart —and not just what I can do for him sexually, he'll ask me on a date. He'll make an effort, make plans, and make an investment to spend time with me. My time is valuable, my energy is a gift, and my presence is palpable. The expenditure doesn't have to be financial, like an expensive dinner-and-drinks date; but no doubt, there's a price. Some of my favorite first dates have been coffee dates or hiking/walking excursions. In these cases, there's little-to-no money spent. Instead, the offering of attention, time, and communication is far more important and treasured in my eyes.

When someone approaches me without offering something in return, like their true selves, I'm not the least bit interested. These advances are simply ignored like the catcallers on the street who shout out as I walk by. If someone wants my attention and desires to date me, I appreciate when they make the effort, share their heart, get to know me, and make plans. Reservations are even better! Basically, I'm looking for substance and value. Without it, I'm either reluctant or I refuse to engage. Here's why: my abundant mindset affirms potential dates are a dime a dozen. Instead of engaging with every person who shows interest, I ignore or release each person who doesn't make an effort or show up with value out of the gate.

*"The difference between successful people and really successful people is that really successful people say no to almost everything."*
—WARREN BUFFETT

# CHAPTER FOUR

## AN ATTRACTIVE "NO"

In the last chapter, Tiffany's response explained that establishing standards, owning your value, and preparing for more aligned options is a powerful key to creating abundance. It sets you up for the professional success you want. She brilliantly made an analogy to relationships because the same standards apply in relationships as in our business endeavors. There's an underlying message that I want to highlight because I think it's important. It's this: creating abundance means getting comfortable saying "No," managing the discomfort that often comes from the perceived rejection of "No," and staying true to the ever-increasing standards you've established for yourself and your business.

All combined, these choices help build sheer personal and entrepreneurial power.

Before I learned my worth and utilized my abundance mindset, I had a friend caution me about how I'd spread myself so thin and give nearly everyone I encountered premium access to my space and time. Sadly, this was true on the business front as well as the personal one. I had a really hard time saying "No" and I honestly didn't understand the power of discernment, deciding who I should give attention to, and how to differentiate the amount and type of attention I gave to different people. I was basically giving everyone I met my "all" and wondering why I was feeling used and exhausted at the end of the day. In other words, I was "easy." We'll talk later about how business owners use discernment and differentiation through the funnels they build and how they create ease of connection without being "easy." For now, I want to talk about how using certain tools along with the power of "No" can not only be attractive, but also create more demand.

Would you rather date someone who has a one-night stand every weekend, or someone who is more discriminating with their intimate endeavors? What about business owners who contract with every Tom, Dick, and Harry? I've even seen leaders in the coaching industry liken giving everyone equal access to do business with them as being similar to being a prostitute who walks the streets. Personally, I believe everything has its place, including prostitution, but the point still stands. Individuals who value their time, alignment, and commitment say "No" more frequently than they say "Yes"—especially when it comes to sexual advances and demands on their time. They simply won't make themselves available for anything less than the highest manifestation of what they desire. Women who want a husband won't date people who want the benefits of a marriage without the commitment. Personally, I'd rather be single than be in a relationship that doesn't serve me on all levels. I've been there, done that. These days, I'm choosing not to accumulate anymore T-shirts stamped with "I settled."

Settling, for me, comes from a lack of faith, low self-worth, and a long-standing pattern of codependency. When I show up in my power and understand my worth, it's easy to be more discerning and not give in—or "give it up"—to every man who wants my attention. Saying "No" also creates additional intrigue and interest with potential dates. A similar situation happens in the business world with clients and prospecting. People want to know you're "in demand," but not "easy." You're "easy" when you neglect maintaining your standards, settle for less than you deserve, and go against your own intuition.

I've always considered myself as a person of high integrity, but in 2020, a mentor introduced a concept of integrity I'd never considered. He said, "Integrity is moving at the speed of your spirit." He went on to say that every time I discounted my spirit and went against my intuition to be "easy" for someone and promote their agenda over mine, I was out of integrity. Before that discussion, I'd considered integrity as external to me and something that's entered into on behalf of others. Putting myself at the center of the integrity equation put an entirely different spin on things. Many thanks to Kyle Lipton for this gem of wisdom.

Even if you've been easy in the past, and accepted clients, dates, or lovers who weren't a perfect match, it's never too late to be more selective and discerning. In the past, I've frequently been the girl who said "Yes" when I should've said "No." Many times over, the "Yes" came in the form of giving in and people-pleasing, and nearly every infraction went against my better intuition. Every time I caved in a transaction I'd likely have said "No" to, it eroded part of my self-esteem, set me up for a negative experience, and established a code of conduct that didn't agree with my soul. For example, as a writer, one of the personal lines I draw is that I only write under my name. Early in entrepreneurship, I did a bit of ghostwriting. No matter how well paid the job was, I was always left feeling unsettled and slighted. This discomfort is the exact reason I should've said "No." However, because I was new to the entrepreneur scene and looking for the experience, I caved and accepted nearly every job offered.

On the other hand, once I established a high value for myself and my services, it was much easier to disregard interactions with others who either didn't have high standards for themselves or didn't see or appreciate the value I had for myself. It's very hard to offer a clear "Yes" or "No" to a partner when you're not saying "Yes" to your own needs and saying "No" to things that don't fit your vision. Alternatively, having a clear vision you're dedicated to makes it very easy to determine what's for you and to disregard what's not.

When collaborating with a client, I experienced what an attractive "No" looks like from a client's perspective. I was looking to provide a new vendor for a client who'd outgrown my services and needed someone to take his business in a different direction. I chatted with an agency owner who told me he turns down 95% of the people who want to do business with him. Why? Because he wanted to maintain his 100% client satisfaction rank along with his own personal satisfaction level. To this agency owner, it didn't matter how much a client was willing to pay, if working with that client could cause headaches or blemish his perfect record. When either of those scenarios felt likely, the agency owner's answer was an automatic "No." Before accepting a new client account, he ensured he could deliver results, the client did their part to achieve the expected results, and there was a personal resonance. Knowing the principles he'd established and adhered to only made me want to work with him even more. I loved the fact that he was protecting both his sense of personal peace and the reputation of his agency in every decision. There had to be a near-perfect match before he moved forward with a contract. In other words, his agency was not "easy." This guy's experience, coupled with the way he used discernment and an attractive "No," created magnetic desire —instantly.

*"Success is a numbers game."*
— JIM ROHN

# CHAPTER FIVE

## IT'S A NUMBERS GAME
### WITH FEATURED AUTHOR JESSE PANAMA

The happy daters I know put themselves out there. They attend events, chat up strangers in line at the grocery store, and are generally open to opportunities in whatever ways they show up. In essence, they're creating a larger pool of numbers to work from. They understand that the more they put themselves out there, the greater chances they have to find their person. At the same time, it's clear that finding people to date, kiss, and have relations with takes sorting through a large number of connections before finding quality ones and agreeing to connect with them.

We've all heard the adage, "You have to kiss a lot of frogs to find your prince," especially when it comes to dating and finding "the one." According to a study commissioned by London dating app Meeteez, "Women kiss 22 people, have four long-term relationships, and get their heart broken five times before they meet 'the one.' They also have on average six one-night stands, get dumped four times, and dump someone five times."[1]

Personally, I think those stats are woefully underrepresented. Considering the societal pressure to "lockdown" our mate for life before the age of 30, I've had more opportunities to kiss frogs in my half-century of life. Or maybe that's just me—especially given my maturity level and the fact that I've yet to meet "the one." LOL.

For one week, and for my own personal edification, I kept track of my numbers from three different dating apps to drive home the point of the sheer number of exposures and impressions that take place before connecting with—and kissing—potential suitors.

Here's a summary of the results:

- Number of suitors who liked me ..............................................43
- Number of suitors I liked ...........................................................2
- Number of suitors I matched with..............................................3
- Number of matches I exchanged dating site messages with.....5
- Number of matches I exchanged texts with ..............................3
- Number of matches I chatted with on the phone with .............3
- Number of matches I went on a first date with.........................2
- Number of matches I went on a second date with....................1

I did kiss two of these frogs and neither of these matches or dates are on my radar these days. Considering that 45 likes resulted in THREE matches, that's less than a 7% chance of even matching, let alone making it through dating site messages, texts, phone calls, and dates to get to the kiss. Yeah, dating is definitely a numbers game. While forever hopeful, I've yet to find my prince.

My numbers above represent only one possible way to meet people— through dating apps. In reality, there's an excess of other avenues to meet people, which rapidly increases these numbers and the chance for true connection.

Business connections are no different. There are an infinite number of ways to connect with potential clients and there's definitely a sorting and qualifying process before moving forward with good candidates.

Client prospecting is like dating. Consider introductory calls as first dates. Just remember that not everyone you have a date with is someone you'll kiss, continue to date, or go to bed with. Frequent prospecting and soliciting clients helps to increase the pool of potential matches and the greater the chance you'll find "the one."

When increasing your pool, you can cast a wide net and waste a lot of time trying to find "your people." Or, you can reduce the frustration and exhaustion caused by haphazard net-casting methods by engaging in some specificity. It's ok to be picky and discriminate. You can be very targeted in your approach, ensuring only those you want to connect with find you. In dating, you can do this by controlling your dating profile settings, being specific about your needs, and putting yourself in target-rich environments where like-minded people convene. In business, this level of specificity is controlled through mining the demographics, ad settings, retargeting, and pixels. Just as you wouldn't waste time or effort promoting your dating profile to people with a different sexual orientation, location, or family status than you prefer, you certainly wouldn't waste ad dollars sharing your business offer to individuals who don't have a natural inclination toward the product or service you provide.

I have a friend and collaborator named Jesse Panama. His business platform is dedicated to a methodical approach for finding an audience that's predisposed to purchase exactly what an entrepreneur has to offer. All the while, the methodology is designed to connect a community of strangers, facilitate heartfelt connections, and develop bonds like a family. You'll hear more about Jesse and his approach to freedom and his company, Ultimate Vida, throughout the book. For now, I've asked him to share an overview of targeting audience members, creating an ecosystem, and coupling them with organic and paid marketing. Here's what he has to say:

*What if instead of slogging through a bunch of frogs to find your prince, we could effortlessly bring forth a harem of princes who are dying to passionately kiss you?*

*And while finding "the one" is presumably the end game in love and dating, in business, we get to practice "ethical non-monogamy" and attract thousands upon thousands of "soulmate clients," customers, and community members.*

*So, what are the two counterintuitive ways we do this?*

*First, we actively cast a narrow net rather than a wide one. Trying to be all things to all people is business suicide. The idea is to create an avatar in vivid detail which represents our ideal community member; and then stack interests, behaviors, and demographics on top of each other to find as many real-life representations of the said avatar as possible—while simultaneously weeding out those who are not your princes!*

*Crucially, we do not do this through guesswork or intuition. While your personal knowledge of your audience is certainly a good place to start, the key is to validate (or invalidate!) this knowledge through the proprietary Ultimate Vida research method.*

*Once we're clear on exactly whom we're targeting?*

*We then make our second counterintuitive chess move of focusing on paid traffic rather than organic. Before you think I've gone stark raving mad, let's unpack for a moment why I strongly suggest—no, implore—you to pay for your traffic rather than get it for "free."*

*First of all, time is money and time is the most precious commodity we've got. So, if you're spending your valuable time creating organic content to (hopefully) attract people to your content—with no ability to target, I might add—is it actually free?*

*With paid traffic, you just put one relevant story or message in front of your target audience—whom you're able to select with laser-precision, I might add—and your princes self-select and come forward automatically, 24/7, even while you're asleep!*

*Sure, this option costs some money. But does it really? Let's think about it. If the idea is to eventually be profitable, is it really a cost?*

*Or is it simply an investment until you get your campaigns dialed in so that for every dollar you spend, you get back $2 or $3 or $5? You'll certainly never achieve this level of predictable results with organic reach!*

*So, go forth, laser-target, pay to play, and watch your charming princes flock to you!*

*"To be yourself in a world that is constantly trying to make you something else is the greatest accomplishment."*
— RALPH WALDO EMERSON

# CHAPTER SIX

## LIVING YOUR BEST LIFE

The last chapter's featured author, Jesse Panama, and I met in 2017 in a Facebook group for digital nomads. He was a presenter for an upcoming conference, teaching budding entrepreneurs his unique method to create wealth and live their best life. "Vida" is Spanish for life, and his company's name is Ultimate Vida. I understood it to be a pure and fun way to live life. When Jesse and I met, I was packing the house I'd owned for 20 years in Des Moines, Iowa, and preparing to start my own version of the "pure life" in the Los Angeles basin of California. You see, I didn't just change my career status from "corporate employee" to "entrepreneur." No, I was in the midst of a massive life change, uprooting myself from the only home I'd ever known in search of the life and work that really resonated with me. While I wasn't exactly sure what that life and work would look like, I was certain of one thing: California was absolutely the place I wanted to create and live my new life. When people ask me why I moved, the answer is always the same: I love the way I *feel* in California. It's a completely different vibe. Of course, the SoCal weather is amazing, but what I love most is how unique and strange people, places, and circumstances are here. It seems that everyone is an entrepreneur, and no matter what you want to do, no matter how strange your pursuits are, you can do it. Even better, you're never alone. You can literally do just about anything you want, and there's a whole bunch of other people doing the same thing. Choosing to move to California was the start of my "Ultimate Vida," I just didn't realize it at the time.

Here's the manifesto Jesse uses to describe the Ultimate Vida:

YOUR NEW LIFE OF ABSOLUTE FREEDOM STARTS RIGHT NOW AND

# IT'S CALLED THE ULTIMATE VIDA
[ IT'S BOTH ART AND A SCIENCE; MAGICAL YET METHODICAL ]

THE ULTIMATE VIDA IS OUR JOURNEY TO FREEDOM AND OUR DESTINATION FROM WHICH WE OPTIMIZE OUR LIVES AND SELF-ACTUALIZE

**IT'S YOUR PLATFORM TO SHINE YOUR BRIGHTEST LIGHT TO GIVE THE WORLD YOUR BEST AND HIGHEST SELF**

IN OUR ULTIMATE VIDA, WE LIVE IN **GRATITUDE, INQUIRY & SERVICE**

WE TRAVEL *INWARDLY* AND *OUTWARDLY* AND OUR LIVES ARE *FOREVER ENRICHED* BY DOING SO

WE EMBRACE OUR *UNITY* AND CELEBRATE OUR *DIVERSITY*

**WE *BUILD WEALTH, GIVE GENEROUSLY* AND *RECEIVE ABUNDANTLY***

[ WE FIND STRENGTH IN OUR VULNERABILITY ]

**WE LOVE PASSIONATELY, LAUGH HEARTILY AND CREATE BREATHTAKING MEMORIES**

WE ARE A WORLDWIDE TRIBE OF BROTHERS AND SISTERS WHO ALWAYS HAVE EACH OTHER'S BACK

**THE ULTIMATE VIDA IS YOUR LIFE'S WORK AND LEGACY**

**YOUR MASTERPIECE—YOUR MAGNUM OPUS**

# ULTIMATE
*Vida*

I was so intrigued by the concept of Ultimate Vida, I asked Jesse to meet me personally when I arrived in California. We met for dinner and drinks at Seal Beach and talked about everything under the sun. Nothing was off limits. I felt so comfortable with him and I knew he'd always be a friend I could count on.

Jesse and I kept in touch over the years, meeting on occasion to swap stories and strategies. He'd been building his business, Ultimate Vida, and literally traveling all over the world doing it. The concept of living the Ultimate Vida, particularly the travel part, has always been a desire of mine. Moving from the Midwest to California to follow my dreams was definitely a great start to creating my own Ultimate Vida.

In 2020, when Jesse was ready to publish his book, *The Art of Freedom*, I was honored to be his publishing partner and sign him as a client. Working with the book really expanded my interest in Jesse's concepts; I was excited by the book's prospects. Even the graphic designer we worked with on the book said, "This guy is a genius, btw." I was truly honored to play a part in helping to put Jesse's ideas into the hands of people who could really use them.

Later, Jesse ran a beta version of his book's teachings as a course with even greater detail, and he offered the course to me as a gift. I wasn't quite ready for it at the time; my life was in a major transition. While I'd created a beautiful life in California, my business prospects weren't going so well. In fact, I was very unstable—emotionally, physically, and financially—and the 2020 pandemic hitting certainly didn't help. In my less-than-optimal state, the idea of my Ultimate Vida seemed like an alternate reality that I hadn't lined up with yet.

A few months later, after I'd done significant training and healing through neuro-linguistic programming (NLP), I reached out to Jesse about the course. I offered my services to help him take the Ultimate Vida course from its beta status to a useable, super scaled-up version. We started collaborating immediately, and that's when I learned the real "secret" to the Ultimate Vida.

In the book, Jesse talked about love being the biggest competitive advantage in business. I was so in alignment with that message; I shot out an article about it for *Entrepreneur* magazine. Even still…

> *It's one thing to read and write about*
> *experiencing love in business,*
> *It's another thing to actually receive it.*

Living and working in the Ultimate Vida method is an entirely new way for me to do business. It's showing up as I am; imperfection, flaws, issues, and all. There's no need to leave who I am at the door in order to do business. Every part of the experience adds to the value of my work. And this entire process is possible for anyone; for everyone. I remember the first time I apologized to Jesse for being "unprofessional" and swearing, something that comes very naturally to me. He replied that I was welcome to speak freely and remarked that swear words can be great sentence enhancers. I think my favorite thing Jesse ever told me is, "Your heart and soul and professionalism are enormous assets to me and Ultimate Vida." The compliment was important for me to hear because when it came to business, my professionalism is a given. But Jesse's recognition of my heart and soul was unprecedented, particularly in the corporate world where I toiled for 25 years. I also value how much he appreciates the unique skills I offer my clients. As an empath working from my heart and soul, that recognition means the world to me.

I can't tell you the freedom I feel as an entrepreneur, building my projects and being my quirky, foul-mouthed self, wearing my heart on my sleeve. When Jesse was my client and I helped him publish his book, *The Art of Freedom*, I told him my job was to hold him to the highest possible vision for his book. I felt it was my duty to challenge him to go higher than he thought possible. Later, when I became an Ultimate Vida client, Jesse reciprocated the sentiment and intention, telling me *he* would hold *me* to the highest vision for my life and business. I believe that's what we're here to do as people and business owners, and I'm elated to be collaborating with someone who has made it their life's mission to help others live their Ultimate Vida.

The world is full of mediocre jobs and businesses that pay the bills but don't feed our souls—or worse, contribute to personal decline through increased stress and health complications. I know this experience intimately. It would seem by the nightly news (which I never watch) and the discontent expressed daily on social media that very few people are living their dream lives. Many business owners believe their businesses must be governed by outdated rules and siloed to keep their work separate from their personal needs and dreams. I've experienced first-hand the way doing business from the heart changes things. I've also experienced the opposite. One gives life, and the other stifles it.

The Ultimate Vida is a life-giving business endeavor. It's about working from a place of joy, pursuing our passions, connecting intimately with others, and making our own world better while inviting others along for the journey. And yeah, there's plenty of money in it, too. And while money is not exactly an afterthought, it's more of a natural occurrence that begins flowing as Jesse's concepts are studied and embraced.

Jesse's client and my new friend Sue has the best story about the natural abundance and personal evolution that occurs when we utilize the Ultimate Vida business model. I'll clue you in later, but for now, know that in a few short weeks of using the model, Sue's new business started generating over $10k a month effortlessly. She immediately quit the full-time job that was consuming her, trading in its "security" for more freedom, peace, and connection.

For me, freedom is the biggest key to living my best life!

*"Wholeness is not achieved by cutting off
a portion of one's being,
but by integration of the contraries."*
—CARL JUNG

# CHAPTER SEVEN

## IT'S ALL RELATED—INTEGRATE IT!

In early 2001, I worked with my then-employer, a third-party-administrator of insurance products, to launch a Business Integration Team. Known as BIT for short, our tagline was "It's all related—integrate it!" The team was founded and funded in an effort to increase the efficiency and profitability of our marketing efforts. Working as a marketing business analyst, I found the departmental silos that made up our organization were truly preventing our marketing team from generating the most successful direct mail marketing offers. Here's why: we didn't communicate, we didn't establish expectations, and we didn't create feedback loops to evaluate and respond to discrepancies in our expected results.

To achieve our mission of greater profitability and efficiency, BIT created cross-departmental communication circles. Through the discussions I facilitated, it was clear our various departments didn't understand how actions in one part of the organization were negatively impacting the other parts. For example, the marketing team could send out a great direct mail package and generate tons of responses. However, the fulfillment, customer service, and accounting teams weren't aware of the mailing, so they weren't prepared to deal with the incoming volume and delays and mistakes were inevitable. Worse, they had no awareness that their specific actions impacted the company's profitability. So, the marketing results suffered. The finger-pointing and blaming for the poor results then created interdepartmental animosity and frustration which, of course, didn't help matters. Once we dug in and researched the company's inefficiencies, it was clear team members were acting from a place of innocent ignorance; they simply didn't know what they didn't know. After we created opportunities for the departments to interact with one another, documented the entire process from beginning to end, and communicated a new set of cooperative expectations, not only did our profitability improve, but employee morale and teamwork did, too.

As an employee trainer with that same company, I would show customer service representatives a single, yellow piece of a kid's puzzle. I'd ask them, "What is this and what's the story that goes with it?" The answers were hilarious and varied, ranging from a lemon, to the sun, to even some unmentionable props. Basically, the trainees were clueless of the big picture based on the single piece I showed them. However, once I showed the cover of the puzzle box and they could see the full picture, their responses were completely different. As soon as they saw the *Sesame Street* characters Bert and Ernie, the yellow puzzle piece made a whole lot more sense—and so did the story.

In order to experience wholeness as individuals, we must understand all the pieces of the puzzle of ourselves, how they fit together, and how to integrate them. It can be challenging to maintain lasting, systemic change when we try to suppress certain parts of our identity or silo them away. Plus, a lack of understanding and communication makes it harder to prevent unintended effects from compartmentalization, just like our corporation's siloed and unintegrated departments destroying our marketing results.

Challenges in relationships, friendships, and home life create challenges in building and maintaining our business. As a result, when there are challenges in the mind, body, and spirit, our business suffers. I recall the first time a businessperson introduced this concept to me. It was 2007, and our insurance company's new Chief Sales Officer gave his first presentation to the staff. The most memorable thing he said to us wasn't about business, goals, or sales tactics. It was, to paraphrase, "I believe in God and I believe in family. Taking care of my relationships with myself, my Creator, and my home allows me to be a productive leader at work." More than the words, it was obvious through his actions that he lived the words he spoke. I visited his home, met his wife, and frequently ran into him at church. He integrated his personal identity with his relationships in a way that enabled him to be present to drive our sales team's success. You can imagine; he was also very personable and relatable and kicked ass when it came to integrating our teams and achieving sales goals.

While I've always prided myself on "walking my talk," I have also experienced major backslides and profound struggles. In 2020, during the historical stressors of the pandemic, some important components of my identity surfaced in a big way. My ego, shadow self, and inner child were running the show and producing the deepest depression and suicidal ideation I'd ever experienced. While I understood these aspects of myself, I was in denial about the depth of their impact, and I hadn't taken the time to address and integrate them properly. In the years prior, I'd invested thousands of dollars in coaching in an attempt to embody my beliefs. I wanted to maintain that fearless part of me who went after what she wanted, focused intently, and had fun along the way. I wanted to tap into the energy of the woman I once was, the one who packed up everything and drove halfway across the country to Southern California on a whim and a prayer. But no matter how enjoyable and effective the coaching programs would be, I had extreme difficulty keeping up with the daily activities needed to maintain the initial progress I enjoyed. No matter how much I'd transform, I kept reverting to old patterns of behavior. This inability to keep my footing knocked me on my ass, and I knew there was more to the story than not having enough willpower to keep on keeping on.

When an opportunity presented itself for me to enroll in a neuro-linguistic programming (NLP) training program, I took a major leap. NLP uses a series of processes designed to align one's mind (neuro), language (linguistic), and actions (programming) and provides tools to keep them aligned to support greater happiness and attract opportunities for abundance through synchronicity. An NLP breakthrough includes a series of tools to address negative emotions, limiting beliefs, and integrate traumatic parts of our psyche that cause internal conflicts. Through the program and my experience of a personal breakthrough, I began to see these puzzle pieces of myself more clearly. At the time, I was drowning in negative emotions and limiting beliefs. Barely able to function, life throughout 2020 was a moment-to-moment exercise in staying alive. Completing the intense 14-week NLP transformation curriculum enabled me to literally change the tapes of my subconscious mind and rewire my brain to properly address the trauma that impacted my ego and inner child triggers. It was also integral in deepening the shadow work that was presented in early 2020. According to psychologist Carl Jung, who coined the concept "shadow work," it's essential to integrate the parts of ourselves we may have deemed "dark" and/or repressed in order to experience wholeness. Jung's famous quote, "Until you make the unconscious conscious, it will direct your life and you will call it fate," was certainly true in my life. My unconscious mind, ego, and inner child were overwhelmed with trauma, limiting beliefs, and negative emotions, and those unaddressed parts within me clouded every single decision in my life.

Two of my favorite tools learned in NLP were the removal of negative emotions and limiting beliefs. Even better than learning them, though, experiencing them produced an immediate and palpable change in my demeanor. One of the coolest things about these particular NLP processes is that they address both ancestral/genetic events as well as past life experiences—without having to revisit, address, or regurgitate any of the trauma and drama. In particular, the negative emotions of shame and guilt—which originated in utero and through previous generations—had a hold on my body and mind since conception. Being born into a family of daughters after a baby boy died at birth, knowing I was an accident, and my mother being sick and on bed rest throughout her pregnancy automatically instilled the shame of never being enough and not being wanted. I instinctively felt like I had to earn my right to exist in the world and spent my life proving my worthiness to avoid the guilt of existing in a family where I wasn't welcomed. Shame and guilt had been unbearable influences throughout my life.

I could feel a difference in my body when the emotion of guilt was removed. However, the removal of shame invited both a sense of peace and ownership of my place in the family and on this earth. For the first time ever, I understood the value of being born as a woman. My body was suddenly activated and "turned on." Yes, literally. Suddenly, I intimately understood the power of being born a woman and having the ability to give LIFE to damn near anything and everything—not to mention birthing the most amazing son.

As remarkable as removing negative emotions was, the real NLP showstopper of my transformation was the parts-integration process. This process allows the student to address parts of themselves with conflicting views, which are creating internal conflict. Common parts to integrate are ones like, "Part of me wants to be successful and rich. Part of me wants to watch Netflix and spend money." Or, "Part of me wants to be healthy, and part of me wants to eat bonbons all day." While the parts-integration process is powerful regardless of which parts are being integrated, the conflicting parts addressed in *my* personal breakthrough were as deep as they could possibly go. The parts-integration process unified the conflicting internal loops of my brain that declared "Part of me feels unworthy to exist" (hence the suicidal ideation) and "I'm here for a reason." Healing occurs through relating the conflicting parts, revealing the higher purpose for the conflict, gathering the learnings to understand the value of the experience and gaining new perspective, and developing self-acceptance by merging the conflicting parts. Clearly, seeing, addressing, and understanding the value of the hardships I'd endured made me grateful.

There were 30 other professionals enrolled in the program with me. Having my whole NLP cohort chant in unison, "You are whole, you are complete, and you are loved," was music to my fragile and recovering nervous system. The crescendo of the parts integration experience was a message from my NLP buddy and wise shamanic mentor, Luis Cerda that tied everything together for me. Luis posted the following statement in the Zoom chat welcoming me home to me and my purpose:

> *Welcome, Melissa! You now have the opportunity to walk into and stand in the totality of who you came here to be, the truth of who you now know yourself to be, and the clarity of mind to peer into existence and know that your place is here; inextricably, lovingly, joyously, among us.*

The result of the process was steady ownership of who I am as a person and a stronger desire to do the work I came here to do. Each week, my NLP classmates saw me show up and be challenged in the most extensive way. I cried relentlessly through the triggers and wanted to quit the program more times than I could count. No matter how much I was challenged, I continued to show up and do the work my NLP program required. My cohort saw the change in me, and toward the end of the program, I began to accept work projects again after being so emotionally distraught that I hadn't completed any paid work in nine months. One of my classmates hired me to assist with his brand development and book writing process. I was excited and a bit nervous, but standing in my "I'm here for a reason" power. I knew I could help him, and I did. I showed up as myself, and we related as friends. I thanked him for hiring me and trusting me—especially after what he'd just seen me go through. He noted, "I trust you more *because* of what I just witnessed."

His statement warmed my heart and allowed me to breathe a big sigh of relief. Those unintegrated parts of myself were nothing to be ashamed of. In fact, the more I shamed them and tried to hide them away, the further I got away from my truth and the work I'm here to do. In the same way the corporate organization I worked for struggled with siloed and unintegrated parts, I was suddenly aware of how I'd been avoiding, shaming, and repressing parts of myself. My healing through NLP processes resembled the efficiencies I created through those corporate communication circles. Addressing "problems" with integrity and taking ownership of my personal transformation, and integrating all parts of myself in an honest and resilient way boosted my spirit and enabled me to demonstrate my ability to connect with and help others. I now know for sure that addressing all aspects of a situation and creating continuity among them is an asset in relationships and business, particularly when you do business with whole hearted people.

*"To be fully seen by somebody, then,
and be loved anyhow–this is a human offering
that can border on miraculous."*
—Elizabeth Gilbert

# CHAPTER EIGHT

## AUTHENTICITY AND VULNERABILITY ENCOURAGED

I make it a point to surround myself with compassionate humans, so the fact that my client and NLP classmate saw me fully wasn't exactly a miracle. As a result of the soul-baring exercises we undertook in the class, he saw and heard more about my life experience than I would've preferred. However, not only did he love me anyway, he trusted me *more* because of our shared experience and our mutual vulnerability in the class. Experiences and interactions like these are more of a norm than a miracle in my world. However, as I've mentioned before, that level of authenticity and vulnerability is not especially encouraged or integrated into the corporate office culture, in my experience.

I've found authenticity and vulnerability absolutely essential for deep and resonant connection. It doesn't matter if that connection occurs as an entrepreneur, a friend, or a love interest. If you're wondering about the first step in becoming authentic and vulnerable, it's simple: tell the truth. It's particularly effective when it comes to telling the truth about your own story. Is it terrifying? Yep. But being afraid is part of the process, according to the author and founder of Mindvalley, Vishen Lakhiani. In his book, *The Buddha and the Badass: The Secret Spiritual Art of Succeeding at Work,* he qualifies this, stating, "Vulnerability is uncomfortable. That's why it's hard. If you think you're doing it right but you don't feel scared, you're not doing it at all. Fear is a prerequisite."

Because I work with coaches and authors to help them write and publish their stories, I often encounter people who are afraid to tell the full truth. I don't think they're actually afraid to tell the truth, but when they write, not many are willing to tell the FULL truth or really go deep. No matter how transparent we are, we're are guilty of it—including me. This is evidenced by the repeated notes from my editor to go deeper, share more, and stop using broad strokes to tell the story. Like me, most authors are particularly afraid of the dark stuff. While that's certainly understandable given fear as a requirement for authenticity, I always encourage them to share as much as they can for this reason: vulnerability invites connections. Every single person has experienced darkness in their lives. The unhealthy thing is that very few people talk about it. Prominent author and expert on vulnerability, Brené Brown, notes the value of sharing the truth stating, "People who wade into discomfort and vulnerability and tell the truth about their stories are the real badasses." I couldn't agree more. Do you know why they are badasses? Because telling the truth opens up space for other people to say "Me, too." When that happens, there's an instant connection, and suddenly authors and readers no longer feel alone in their darkest thoughts and experiences. Now there's an opportunity for further dialogue, connection, and understanding. What's more, these conversations, connections, and understanding can create change.

*There's no time greater than now to initiate change—and lasting change begins with relationships.*

Early in my career, I learned the business word was logical and cold, which is the opposite of personal relationships. Relationships and businesses can and should be warm, intimate, and heartfelt. Dare I say the best business ventures cultivate connection and love among their team members and client base? This kind of cultivation enables relationships with clients in their heart space and meets them on their level, wherever that level is. Here's the thing, we experience the most triggers in relationships. To effectively manage triggers, it's important to witness another's process, take personal accountability for my part of the interaction, and avoid blame. When this is done, relationships serve as the greatest opportunities for growth. Considering we spent at least one-third (more like two-thirds for entrepreneurs) of our time working, our business can serve the same kind of function—triggers can be acknowledged, addressed and treated with compassion.

When I share vulnerable thoughts, about business and in a business setting, I often feel like Jerry Maguire as he was typing a manifesto called "The Things We Think and Do not Say—The Future of Our Business." In the 1996 Tom Cruise movie *Jerry Maguire*, Jerry, a prominent sports agent, has what appears to be an intuitive download about a better way to do business. His ideas were unconventional, much like those in this book. Plus, his suggestions completely bucked the materialistic system that created his success. The through line of his message, which in one crucial scene, he put into a rambling and vulnerable mission statement drafted in the middle of the night, goes like this:

> *Let us start a revolution. Let us start a revolution that is not just about basketball shoes, or official licensed merchandise. I am prepared to die for something. I am prepared to live for our cause. The cause is caring about each other. The secret to this job is personal relationships.*

Rather than being praised for speaking up and attempting to create a revolutionary new paradigm, Jerry Maguire was promptly fired. On his way out of the office with his tail between his legs and a single box of belongings in his arms, office assistant Dorothy, played by Renée Zellweger, joined him. Personally aligned with Jerry's message, Dorothy walks out and joins Jerry's new, more heartfelt way of doing business. While most of his clients held tightly to the corporate paradigm, which disregarded personal relationships, Jerry retained one special client. As a client, Rod Tidwell, played by Cuba Gooding, Jr., bought into Jerry's new approach. In this book, I'm very much relaying the things I think that are not frequently spoken. However, the main difference between Jerry Maguire and me is, I've already had my departure from the corporate world. I've also reached the point where I have clients like Rod Tidwell, who tell me, "I dig that about you!" when addressing my unique style of relating to business.

My most Jerry Maguire-esque moment happened a few months before my corporate position was eliminated. After a long and arduous collaborative effort, we were about to release the company's first newsletter for seniors who enrolled in our Medicare supplement insurance products. After months of personally leading and managing every component of the newsletter from scratch, including writing, designing, and editing the work of other contributors, it was time to show the newsletter off. We partnered with a well-known ad agency in town and asked them to give us some feedback on it before the launch. In advance of the meeting, and likely expecting some criticisms of my work, my CEO boss was quick to preempt my potential triggers by saying, "So if you're sensitive that day, do something so you won't be sensitive." In all honesty, the work was solid, and so was I. To this day, I count that newsletter as some of the best work I've ever delivered. I wasn't the least bit concerned about what the ad agency execs had to say because I knew any feedback they had would serve to improve the end result. But the fact that my boss anticipated an uncomfortable trigger, and then told me to suppress my feelings (and potentially drug or numb myself to them), was disheartening. By the way, the ad team had nothing but praise for the project, and everyone left the meeting with smiles and high fives—including me and the CEO.

While I avoided a potential trigger back then, I'm still not impervious to them. I'm a very emotional person, deeply connected to my work. When an untimely trigger made me cry unexpectedly during a business call with Jesse about our Ultimate Vida work, he said, "Ok, let's give space to release whatever is coming up." We then took the space and time to address my concern before jumping into our project work. Having space to express and be held during that process was completely different than being told to suppress and avoid emotion at work. While I was initially surprised by Jesse's support of my emotional state, I've come to appreciate and admire it. Often, you'll find me channeling *my* inner Rod Tidwell frequently telling *him*, "I dig that about you!"

Isn't that kind of affirmation what we all want? Doesn't everyone want to have their unique expressions seen, heard, and appreciated? In reality, this isn't necessarily an easy or effortless process for me and includes a few considerations. First, it requires expressing myself in a way that's unique and particular to my life experiences without fear or the need to suppress or repress parts of who I am. Next, it's doing so in a space and with people who create safety and allow for such expression without putting a box around it, shutting it down, or shaming it. Finally, it's orienting my relationships with people who appreciate and celebrate who I am as a person and support my continued growth.

*"Content builds relationships.*
*Relationships are built on trust.*
*Trust drives revenue."*
—ANDREW DAVIS

# CHAPTER NINE

## COURTSHIP MATTERS
### WITH FEATURED AUTHOR JESSE PANAMA

Although it does happen—though not always with great success—in my experience, few first dates end in sex. Even fewer relationships that begin with sex end in marriage. In dating and relationships, most people work up to the "big event" of sexual intercourse and control the flow of sexual activities as they spend more time together and pursue a commitment with one another. While there's no hard-and-fast rule of when to take the plunge into having sex, it's best to ensure compatibility, chemistry, and, of course, consent before moving forward. Long-term or exclusive commitment is a bonus, but not necessarily a requirement in today's modern dating world.

What's the best way to gauge compatibility, chemistry, consent, and commitment in dating or relationships? Answer: getting to know one another through experiences and exposing others to our heart and mind through conversations and dates. Instead of jumping into sexual activity and other "entanglements," remaining open and allowing things to unfold organically is a great way to determine if you even *want* to go there with someone new. Often after a few dates, sometimes it's clear that I not only don't want to have sex with this person, but I don't even want to be friends with them so, it's important to stay true to who I am. That means being myself when I date someone new and staying in my own bubble of personal sovereignty. Yes, we can show up for one another, and doing that may create an opportunity to establish or further a relationship. However, I can't go further to please another than I go for myself. Personally, I've had a tendency to automatically attach to the people I date and push for commitment. Unfortunately, like many, I sometimes have done so even before I've ensured my own boxes of compatibility, chemistry, and consent are clearly checked.

In the fall of 2020, I had an aha moment relating the concept of courtship to the struggles I was experiencing in my business. I had two potential clients with needs I could easily manage through my zone of genius: writing, editing, and publishing. When neither of them moved forward and contracted work with me, I was crushed. Much like dating, business leads can be approached as opportunities to experience a service, be exposed to the results, and make a choice regarding the level of commitment that's appropriate. I realized that I was approaching business in the same way I was approaching dates, which was, "let's commit, move in, and get married." For the record, I actually did that once; it didn't work out long-term.

With both of the business proposals, I proposed a high-end publishing package that was more of a partnership in its intensity and involvement. I did this rather than giving the clients what they actually had asked for—an editing service with a manageable rate. There's no question I could deliver on the services I'd proposed; I'd had clients delighted by a more extensive package. However, these were brand new clients I hadn't worked with before. They had no idea what to expect, and I proposed a host of services way beyond what they'd actually asked for. As partners, we were compatible, but we hadn't done any work together to test the chemistry, and most importantly, I didn't have consent to move forward farther than they'd inquired about; I just shot the moon. For these reasons, looking back, it's no surprise they failed to commit.

From this experience, I learned that rather than going "all in" when proposing a business offering and heading straight to an in-depth partnership, it's better to instead go on a "first date;" give them a "taste" of my work—maybe even at an introductory rate. Once I've earned their commitment and initial consent, it's time to wow them. Just like in dating, this is done by getting to know a client's needs, showing up for them, and expanding the relationship through conversation, continued work, and new contracts. It's a delicate dance where we exchange value with one another. I provide a service and they provide payment for the service. As we dance with services, we're building mutual trust through each exchange. Once they're hooked and happy with the service provided, it's much easier to ask for a higher-level contract and work up to the bigger partnerships. Also, their happiness and social proof in the form of a testimonial makes it easier to magnetize new clients and keep existing ones coming back for more while ensuring my name is at the top of their referral list.

What's the best way to gauge compatibility, chemistry, consent, and commitment in entrepreneurship and business-building? Answer: getting to know one another through experiences and exposing clients to my business methods and approach through deepening business transactions. Instead of jumping into partnerships and other "entanglements," doing business repeatedly and allowing things to unfold organically is a great way to determine if I even *want* to partner with someone new.

Working on a project with Jesse, the leader of Ultimate Vida, further distinguished the idea of incremental client "advancement" in my mind. As we were setting up my ecosystem to attract authors who need editing and publishing services, I relayed to him that the process of establishing a landing page and email nurturing sequence feels like courtship to me. When courting someone new, you don't go to sex immediately. Yet, immature marketers do it all the time when soliciting business. In the online world, an immediate request for sex sounds something like "buy my fucking product!" It's akin to attempting to go all the way on the first date. Without building systems to truly cultivate relationships with prospects, there's no way they'll engage—let alone go all the way with you as a service provider. In my work with Jesse, I quickly became curious about what it would look like to serve potential clients in a way that creates this magnetized "I want more of that" or "I'll have what she's having" orgasmic response like bystanders in the café experienced when Sally showed Harry what a faked female orgasm looks like in the 1989 romantic comedy *When Harry Met Sally*. Except, I want the real thing—at least, in the business-sense. After I left him a message about the association I'd created in my mind, he quickly responded, stating:

> *I fucking love this message you just left me. We're definitely in sync and operating on a very high level. I so appreciate you being open to tapping into that level because it's yet another example of not doing business in a conventional way and understanding things at an advanced and nuanced level. It's extraordinarily valuable.*

> *Doing business intimately allows us to effortlessly hit all of the conventional benchmarks and metrics we're looking for from a place of instant connection and validation in the form of a powerful and emotional story, starring your reader.*

From there, he went onto explain key tools used in online businesses and the way they relate to dating.

> *Think of a client's courtship journey this way: The landing page is the opening line for the first contact. But it's not a cheesy, stupid pick-up line. It's a very authentic, and radically transparent opening line. Imagine someone breaking the ice in such an unusual, intriguing, and unexpected way that it instantly made you curious in a way that you not only want to know more, you <u>need</u> to know more. Right away, that's where the attraction begins.*

> *When the potential client engages you by joining your ecosystem through your email list, you begin communicating with them. The*

*first thing you do after they subscribe to your email is verify consent through validation and permission. After that, the conversation opens, and the courtship begins. Through this courtship process, you're peeling back the layers, telling stories, and revealing more of the potential journey. Along the way, client engagement, intrigue, and attraction increases.*

*Then, foreplay starts as the attraction and chemistry increases. Here, the romance, the sensuality starts. The idea is for the foreplay to be such a turn-on, such an aphrodisiac, almost drug-like, that the actual buy-in, the "sex," is a foregone conclusion. You don't even think about whether or not you'll consummate this connection. Instead, the answer to nearly every question becomes "Of course!" or "Fuck yes!" Everything has been done in such a thoughtful manner, full of passion, curiosity, vulnerability, and authenticity, that coupling as business partners becomes inevitable.*

Considering a dating profile is the equivalent of a landing page, I'm off to write an intriguing opening line. I'm so ready to connect with a man, get to know his heart, start a courtship, and establish a committed partnership. As Jesse explained, an intriguing opening line, foreplay, engagement, and chemistry creates the forgone conclusion to consummate an entrepreneurial connection too.

*"But the law of magnetism really is true: who you are is who you attract."*
—JOHN C. MAXWELL

# CHAPTER TEN

## ATTRACTION VERSUS PROMOTION

According to Dictionary.com, "attraction" is defined as follows:

1. the act, power, or property of attracting.
2. attractive quality; magnetic charm; fascination; allurement; enticement.
3. a person or thing that draws, attracts, allures, or entices.
4. a characteristic or quality that provides pleasure; an attractive feature.
5. Physics. the electric or magnetic force that acts between oppositely charged bodies, tending to draw them together.
6. an entertainment offered to the public.

If we put the above definitions in a blender, we find that attraction is purposeful, yet it happens without effort. It's fun, light, exciting, and even magical.

Conversely, the Dictionary.com definition of "promotion" is as follows:

1. advancement in rank or position.

2. furtherance or encouragement.
3. the act of promoting.
4. the state of being promoted.
5. something devised to publicize or advertise a product, cause, institution, etc., as a brochure, free sample, poster, television or radio commercial, or personal appearance.
6. also called queening. Chess. the replacement of a pawn that has reached the enemy's first rank by a more powerful piece of the same color, usually a queen.

Just reading the definition of promotion feels like "work" to me. It's full of posturing, and reeks of perfection. It feels heavy and manipulative. Having spent most of my career in marketing, I can tell you that marketing *is* manipulative. There's an intense amount of work behind the scenes in understanding human psychology and using the perfect words, images, and advertisements to promote products and services.

In light of the definition of "promotion" above, it's clear there's an undercurrent at play, one that doesn't bode well for dating or business. It's this: feeling or acting as if you have power over another. Sometimes, that feeling of power comes from a place of superiority and a feeling of being "above" those whose attention you're trying to gain through promotion. Whether that's in the dating pool or the boardroom, superiority doesn't provide lasting results. On the other hand, authenticity and magnetism does. In other words, attraction is a much more effective connection tool.

There's power in attraction, too, except the power in attraction comes from deeds and actions, whereas promotional power is generally garnered from words and appearances. Hence, the truism, "actions speak louder than words." What's more, the feeling that's stirred in the recipient is completely different when they experience words without action vs. when even the same words are backed by action.

Here's how this relates to entrepreneurship and dating. Imagine two different dating scenarios. First, a date who shows up and talks nonstop about how great he is, how much money he makes, and how good he is in bed. He may even have an expectation that because he's "so great" and has "treated" his date to such a great time, that she owes him something. He's coming from a place of entitlement, expecting to get something in return. Well, in business, that's exactly the point.

> *While those on the receiving end of promotion may comply and move forward, it's possible they're doing it out of guilt and obligation rather than inspiration. When this happens, they're not committed from the heart.*

Second, imagine another man who shows up on a date and is completely himself. He may also happen to think he's great, makes a ton of money, and is really good in bed. But rather than spending the date blabbering on promoting himself, he demonstrates his qualities and his character through his actions. He takes the initiative to make reservations, pay for dinner, and connect with his date. He opens car doors, listens attentively, and spends much more time showing interest in his date by asking about them than he does expounding on his own attributes. He's giving of his time and attention with no expectation of a return. My experience is that this man has a much better chance for a later, bigger "return," that is, a lasting, meaningful connection. In other words, he's much more likely to evoke a sensual response from his partner. In fact, in time, there's no question he'll "go all the way" and get laid. Plus, the interaction will come naturally instead of through effort.

Here's the parallel of the above dating scenarios from an entrepreneurial perspective: Almost two decades ago, I took over management of the research department for a large insurance company. Because we needed several surveys and focus groups completed, I began searching for the perfect partner to help us. After reviewing multiple proposals, I asked two finalists to come in for a personal presentation. I hadn't worked with either of the vendors. I was completely in charge of the decision-making, and both prospects were on equal footing in terms of being chosen.

The first, a well-known local vendor, was the research partner my company had used for the past decade. When they came in for the meeting, all they talked about were their credentials, the prior campaigns they completed, and results they'd achieved. Not once did they ask a question about my needs or goals, hence they didn't ask about the insurance company's needs. If they had, they would've learned that those prior campaigns were completely irrelevant to our current projects and goals. There was no question the vendor had the skills and resources to meet my research needs. In fact, I think they thought their past performance was a guarantee of loyalty. However, because they didn't bother to ask about our new projects, or connect with me personally, I had zero attachment to them and was completely dissatisfied with their presentation. They were shocked not to receive the contract they assumed was "in the bag."

In contrast, when Maureen, an out-of-state small business owner with her own firm showed up for our meeting, she was full of questions and was all ears to learn about our needs. She came clearly prepared with a professional presentation, testimonials, and examples of her prior work. However, she didn't lead with that—at all. Instead, she led with her personality, an inquisitive approach, and her ability to make a personal connection with the decision maker—me. I didn't even spend much time reviewing the package she provided with her credentials; the decision was a no-brainer. Maureen was the chosen vendor for our needs. Over time, she became a close friend, an exclusive vendor, and a true partner who helped the insurance company achieve our goals. During the time we worked together, we completed several large projects over many years.

In the above example, the vendor who over-promoted themselves lost a previously loyal client, and the one who connected more personally attracted our insurance company as a newly-loyal client, yielding repeated six-figure contracts. As someone who dates and who also prospects for clients, I've played the part in both of these scenarios, learning from each. I've been the one promoting myself and my services, and I've been one who attracts clients effortlessly by my earnestness and interest. And the results are wildly different. For me, the difference in whether I show up as one who promotes versus one who attracts, boils down to *ownership*. When I'm owning my personal power, tapped into the mindset of abundance, and am certain that the clients (or dates) meant for me will arrive, I attract and magnetize others. From this place, it's easy to be present, in my body, and 100% authentic.

On the other hand, when I'm unsure of myself, it's easier to believe there are a limited number of prospects and to get stuck in a scarcity mindset. When bogged down with that feeling of lack, it's harder to be present and in my body. As a result of not being present, I'm more apt to lead with promotion over authenticity. Fear pushes me to over-promote. The funny thing is, it's in those moments of fear that authenticity and vulnerability can lead to the most heartfelt connection. So, given a choice between attraction and promotion, while feeling the fear, I go further into vulnerability, and create the space to listen to a client's needs and respond in the same way my research partner Maureen so beautifully demonstrated.

*"Healing may not be so much about getting better, as about letting go of everything that isn't you— all of the expectations, all of the beliefs— and becoming who you are."*
—RACHEL NAOMI REMEN

# CHAPTER ELEVEN

## UNVEILING WHOLENESS
### WITH FEATURED AUTHOR JO DECHENNE

In order to let my authenticity shine, create more ownership, and attract better prospects for both my work—and dating—life, I began working with Jo DeChenne. She's a psychic intuitive, and energetic healer who uses telekinesis and light language to move illness, depression, and anxiety out of the body. She's directly connected to archangels, spirit guides, and energies from other realms.

If you're wondering what all this "woo woo" stuff has to do with dating, entrepreneurship, attraction, and promotion, the answer is *everything*. In her own words, I'll let JoJo explain.

> *I met Melissa in the early summer of 2020. What stood out very first in my experience of her was the unimaginable amount of pain and trauma she was carrying around in her internal energy systems. The cry for help was like a living thing within her.*
>
> *We began an incredible journey together on May 29th, 2020, and neither of us has ever looked back. In the months that followed our meeting, she was able to let go of truckloads of trauma (both hers and others she picked up along the way). She went from living in a tumultuous figurative shack built on ever-shifting sands to a grand*

*home built on the bedrock of her transformation. Her dedication was 100% and remains that way today. She's now far closer to a vibrational match to what she most desires.*

*To fully understand Melissa's incredible transformation, I believe you should hear about mine. In facing my own mortality, I magically rediscovered life. I realized I could never take "the little things" for granted again. I healed. In 2018, I started to pick up psychic information from everyone I met. In 2019, I took a trip to Disneyland with my husband and read the book Ask Your Guides by Sonia Choquette. Upon connecting with my first Guide, I knew life was never going to be the same.*

*Almost instantly my days were filling up with people who loved the Guides and what they were capable of doing. In November of 2020, my Guides finally told me what I was. (I secretly thought "freak" was an appropriate title.) Apparently, I was something called a "shaman." I had never heard that word before. The guides absolutely adored my ignorance.*

*I was being taught things at lightning speed and shared all of it with my clients. Word spread and I was so busy come the next January—eight short months after attracting my first client—that I had to start a wait-list.*

*Back to Melissa. As my first paying client, and someone who came to me through a referral, she has been on the journey with me from the beginning. As the world was enduring the violent pandemic of the coronavirus, I was happy to be inside on Zoom working with people and seeing what all these angels and guides could really do.*

*Melissa came to me with treatment-resistant depression and it was serious. She was more than forlorn; she was deeply suicidal. She was dedicated to getting well though, in a way that challenged me. Her dedication pushed the proverbial "Us" harder. We began working with the archangels. If you haven't tried this, I recommend it! These brilliant beings are available to all of us, limitless in power and availability. In serving us, they serve God, and that's their ultimate mission.*

*After a couple months meeting weekly, I began to see a fundamental change in Melissa. She threw her heart and soul into a fantastic NLP program and that, coupled with our work, is what ultimately set her on the journey back to the center of herself.*

*Lately, we've been discussing the vast difference between attraction and promotion. Why it is that some people struggle and struggle to get an idea or a company off the ground, while others seem to do nothing and it falls into their lap? Is this luck? Bad karma? My answer to both questions is a solid, "No." In my very real experience, it's about vibration. Working with energy the way I do, I have a very personal and real knowledge of the Law of Attraction. Why was I able to open a thriving practice only four months after being activated as a shamanic lightworker? I was a retired accountant, for goodness' sake.*

*Here's the thing though; I always knew there was something more I would be doing. I believed in magic. I practiced and studied spiritual matters for most of my life. On my bathroom floor, I vowed to my guide that I would never doubt my Gift if he would blow my mind. Long story short, he absolutely blew my mind and I've never wavered from that commitment. As a result, I was a perfect vibrational match to be the healer I was destined to be. I declared my willingness to believe in the unbelievable, and I received more and more of it. Attraction is magnetic. If we believe 100% in what it is we want and move only in that direction with no room for doubt, we are likely to get all we dream of and more. I'm living proof.*

*Promotion can be tricky. Vibrationally, it can be a struggle. Being an entrepreneur, Melissa knows this better than anyone. The rigors of developing a brand, and an ecosystem (as she calls it) to match, can be a huge undertaking. Essentially, it's not always easy to sell* *yourself—especially if you're experiencing challenges like Melissa was when we met. I feel the most successful people are the ones who truly <u>are</u> themselves. If you show up in a room full of people and you've done your inner work, and have exorcised the personal demons that kicked your ass for years, people are going to see you <u>shine</u>. It's about showing people instead of telling people; About "being" instead of "doing." It's a big concept yet also quite simple.*

*Take Alcoholics Anonymous (AA) for instance. Birthed by two men in 1935 in Akron, Ohio, there are now millions and millions of AA members all over the world. I believe it to be one of the most brilliant examples of attraction-over-promotion of all-time. You have never seen a commercial for AA. Never an advertisement anywhere. Yet, it's simple. The way people change in that program is what makes it so successful. People show up and tell the truth; they become who they truly are. That alone draws others in.*

*To anyone searching for who you are, don't give up. I have actually experienced real magic and know it's a very tangible thing for each and every person who truly believes. So is real healing. You don't have to accept less to scrape by. Quiet your mind. Ask your guardian angel for their name. Wait. See what comes. Your life will never be the same.*

*"The ultimate competitive advantage is love."*
—JESSE PANAMA

# CHAPTER TWELVE

## LOVE IS THE ANSWER

In his book, *The Art of Freedom*, Jesse Panama proclaims that the philosophy of love lends a business its competitive advantage. Though it may seem counterintuitive, his suggestion to run a business with love —yes, love—is actually a quite pragmatic way to approach most endeavors. Jesse sums up the technique simply as, "Treat the people in your market or audience (your community) like family."

If there's one word that describes family—especially the family we choose—it's "love." If there's one phrase that directs businesses, it's "competitive advantage." Given these truths, the question becomes, how does an organization marry "love" with "competitive advantage" to achieve greater satisfaction and produce better bottom-line results? And, is it really important to do so?

Research says, "Yes!" So, let's cover the research confirming the importance of love and happiness in sales. The director of an 80-year study of adult development,[1] George Vaillant, stated, "Happiness is love. Full stop."[2] The study followed Harvard graduates over their life-time and determined that loving relationships are the most prominent indicator of both happiness and income. In addition to strong marriages, the study reported social engagement and support from friends, groups, and volunteer activities as key components of happiness.

If love equals happiness, how does happiness impact business productivity? A 2019 study by the University of Oxford indicates employees are 13% more productive when they're happy.[3] In his book, *The Buddha and the Badass*, Vishen Lakhani recounts his interview with Shawn Achor, author of *The Happiness Advantage*, who detailed the following statistics: "When the brain is in a positive state, productivity rises by 31%, sales success increases by 37%, intelligence, creativity, and memory all improve dramatically. Doctors primed to be happy are 19% better at making the right diagnosis."

The value of facilitating love and happiness as a competitive advantage for greater sales in a professional setting is clear. However, for many—especially traditional corporations—the concept of love, and even happiness, in the office may be a totally foreign concept. Thankfully, it's different in the entrepreneurial space, though—at least for the people I do business with. I honestly feel like we love-minded entrepreneurs belong to one another and our goals and passions are shared. Again, according to Lakhiani, who also founded the personal development company Mindvalley, "When you bring connection to your workplace, you give people and yourself one of the greatest gifts in the world—and the gift with the highest correlation to human happiness. The gift of belonging."

Research by Gallup's Q12 Employee Engagement Survey confirms that people who have a best friend at work are "seven times as likely to be engaged in their jobs, are better at engaging customers, produce higher-quality work, have higher well-being and are less likely to get injured on the job."[4] It's through shared moments that community breeds intimacy, trust, and love in business, in a direct correlation to our private, interpersonal world of dating and relationships.

One of my favorite books is *The Five Love Languages: The Secret to Love That Lasts* by Gary Chapman, PhD. A close work friend suggested I read the book when my son was a toddler over two decades ago. A love language is a means by which we relate intimately with others. The love languages are: words of affirmation; physical touch; acts of service; receiving gifts; and quality time. Understanding them really helped me understand not only the way I feel loved, but how I could love others best and in ways that resonated with them. I honestly consider the love languages in all of my personal interactions, from parenting and family relationships, to friendships, romantic relationships, and client engagements. Last year, on a drive to the beach in San Diego, it hit me that I could apply each of the five love languages to the office as well. I was so excited, I had to pull over and take notes on the ideas that came to me.

I quickly wrote an article with my "take" on translating each of the love languages to workplace scenarios and published it with *Entrepreneur* Magazine. I didn't know it when I wrote the article, but an entire book, strategy, and training program had already been developed to help businesses gain the advantages drawn out of love language research. I sent my article to Appreciation at Work™, the organization established to share the principles of the best-selling book, *The 5 Languages of Appreciation in the Workplace: Empowering Organizations by Encouraging People*. The book and organization are designed to help businesses create healthy workplace cultures and ensure team members feel valued. One of my favorite quotes, and the overall thesis from the book, is "We believe people in the workplace need to feel appreciated in order for them to enjoy their job, do their best work, and continue working over the long haul."

I couldn't agree more! I was grateful to receive a thoughtful reply to my inquiry from Paul White, PhD. As one of the founders and co-authors of the book, he fully embodies its concepts. From the detailed email response he sent, the time he spent connecting with me on the phone, the books he sent me, and his offer to assist me in sharing and promoting my work, I not only felt appreciated, I felt loved when I connected with him.

Given the statistical support of love and happiness as proven means to increase sales in the workplace, there's no question an organizational culture that nurtures employee satisfaction is a logical choice for both the employer and the workforce. Workplace languages of appreciation offer a framework to foster love, self-worth, and connection as one of the greatest competitive advantages an organization can utilize.

Love and appreciation, or lack thereof, is the reason why my friend Linda Gordon left her W2 job to establish her own consultancy business, aptly named Pura Vida Operations. Plus, she found venturing out on her own offered her a greater sense of personal alignment. Even better, she uses self-love as a competitive advantage to connect with and serve her clients. In her own words, here's what Linda had to say about the advantages of entrepreneurship, love, and working on her own terms.

> *Do you know what gives me energy and makes me more productive? Rest, play, scheduled autonomy, trust, and human-centered work environments. Essentially, I garner energy from flexibility and freedom.*

> *Instead of working for the money, I now work for the benefits that matter to me. I work to have the freedom to be me and make work a part of my life, instead of having work represent my whole life.*

> *My health can be annoying, and my mental health needs consistent attention. Being able to manage my energy, take breaks when I need to, and schedule time for rest and play makes all the difference in my personal happiness and alignment.*

> *As an entrepreneur, I feel like I'm living life—and loving it, rather than working my life away.*

> *Every day I can step more into what Pura Vida means to me, which I based my first business around after 10 days in Costa Rica, where I worked and played, and even took surf lessons in-between calls on a Tuesday.*

*Being able to travel and work in beautiful, new temporary offices has been enlightening. It cultivates creativity and even more energy to see new places, meet new people, understand more languages, and learn about new cultures and ways of doing things. It's humbling and freeing while providing time to play and fulfill my inner curiosity for the world.*

*Combining work and play like this has been a dream come true.*

*I know I want my clients to feel better, too. Their passion is what I connect to, and sometimes passion drives business owners to overwork and burn out. In my role, I'm happy to help businesses run better, set some goals that include what they want to feel like and work towards, and leave them feeling more organized and efficient.*

*This problem/solution match created a win-win situation. Work is not draining, and the relationships I can grow with my clients are meaningful, healthy, flexible, and, you guessed it—productive.*

*Since leaving an anchor, the opportunities I have found and aligned to have given me joy, fulfillment, challenge, and motivation. I can be me, choose who I work with, release energy and clients that aren't right for me, and trust that the people I work with love and appreciate me.*

*As an entrepreneur, my relationship with myself has grown exponentially. Because I'm in control of what, when, and where I do business, I'm open to so much personal growth.*

Linda's message really hits home for me. Love most certainly is the answer and the competitive advantage we need to succeed. Love begins first with one's self. Having the time and the ability to truly heal, manage my mental health, and do business on my terms is shaping up to be the best competitive advantage I have—especially when mental health issues previously led me to believe I'd "failed."

*"It is impossible to live without failing at something,
unless you live so cautiously that you might as well
not have lived at all–in which case,
you fail by default."*
— JK ROWLING

# CHAPTER THIRTEEN

## IT'S A PROCESS

In early 2020, I experienced a heartbreak that totally consumed me. While my encounter with this love was unusually brief, it was the most significant and profound "relationship" I'd experienced in California. For the first time, I felt like I'd attracted someone who had the potential be a true partner. It didn't feel like a "situationship," "shituationship," or "playtime" with someone who didn't have their shit together. Instead, I connected with a grown-ass man who was a successful entrepreneur and the most masculine man I'd ever dated. Or maybe more appropriately stated, I'd learned enough about masculine and feminine polarity to recognize and receive his masculinity from a feminine place. He took initiative, made plans and reservations, and communicated openly. He was emotionally available and provided me space to share my full expression—even the scary and vulnerable stuff. You could tell he'd done the work of healing and he wasn't afraid to share what he'd learned. I felt seen. I felt heard. I was safe to express myself vulnerably and did so frequently. I was eager to move forward with him. No doubt, I got excited and attached to him early. Everything felt aligned—until it didn't. When the lack of alignment related to one of my deepest personal wounds occurred, I was crushed.

I immediately called my 25-year-old son Johnathan when this man and I parted ways. I can hardly even call what happened a break-up considering we weren't in a committed relationship in the first place. However, that major detail didn't matter when it came to what my heart was feeling—likely because I was dealing with the personal wound which triggered the end of our budding romance. As I recounted all the ways I screwed up in securing a partnership I desired, my son reminded me that success—whether in life, love, or business—is a process. He said, "Life is a series of fuck-ups and restarts. The key is to fuck-up a bunch. Then you realize how not to fuck-up, and that's how you progress." I'll be damned if he wasn't right! I just may not have wanted to hear it at the time. That's usually the way truth settles with me. First, the truth pisses me off; then, I see the beauty of it. Plus, I felt I'd fucked up enough on the relationship front, and I was so excited to have experienced a totally different beginning in the potential relationship I'd just lost.

My 2020 was off to a good start with a crushing blow to the ego. A few personal fuck-ups under my belt, I went about realizing how *not* to fuck-up so I could progress. When I've been hurt by a rough break-up, it's tempting to go into a shell and never want to date again. However, considering one of my greatest longings is to be in a loving partnership, I knew that staying in my shell and refusing to date wouldn't get me any closer to the partnership I dreamed of. My son and his friends have a saying about jumping into love: "I'm ready to get hurt." Their intention is not to manifest the next break-up, but to have an honest, open understanding that there's always a potential for pain when it comes to love. The pain and the lessons learned from it are part of the process that opens the heart to greater love. There must be a willingness to experience this hurt, sometimes inadvertently expressed as "failure," in order to keep progressing and manifesting the greatest love.

One of my favorite poets, Alfa Holden, addresses the sheer perfection and advantageousness of my son and his friends' saying about love. In a viral meme, Alfa wrote:

*I don't want a heart that's perfect and unused. It won't know how to love me. I want one that's ripped in half. Gaping open. Primed and ready. A heart that has endured a "past" is a warrior. It's been tested and tried and proven to be resilient.*

Starting a business and building it successfully as an entrepreneur are no different than the open-heartedness both my son and the poet Alfa speak to. Starting a business is risky. Sometimes, especially after an unrelenting and unprecedented year like 2020, continuing a business after a great loss might feel even foolish. However, choosing *not* to press on with one's enterprising vision is akin to refusing to date after a breakup. Look, I was in my sixth year as an entrepreneur, and as a result of everything that encompassed 2020, for the first time, I seriously considered closing up shop and working for someone else. I even dusted off my resume and applied for jobs. After everything I'd been through, I wasn't sure I was cut out to continue the path of entrepreneurship.

I'll tell you something that's not talked about often enough: on the way to success, there's often a lot of hurt. With every level of advancement, there are new levels of challenges to confront and demons to vanquish. Growth is painful. Resiliency is one of the greatest currencies an entrepreneur owns. But even the beauty of resiliency is gathered through pain as our comfort zone expands; they're like growing pains. We don't become resilient when everything works out perfectly the first time. We earn resiliency when we fall down, get back up, and start again—over and over. It's the starts and restarts that contribute to our growth. I've had a quote from Mike Dooley, founder of The Universe Talks®, on my refrigerator for more than a decade, which says, "The one thing all famous authors, world-class athletes, business tycoons, singers, actors, and celebrated achievers in any field have in common is that they all began their journeys when they were none of these things." The path to success is paved with opportunities for growth and hard lessons.

Some important components of achieving what's desired as an entrepreneur are beginning strong with a clear vision, understanding what it takes to realize the desired outcome, and showing up in integrity until you reach that goal. Instead of being knocked out by the fuck-ups, we can accept the hurt that comes from fuck-ups, learn from each fuck-up, and progress from one fuck-up to the next. No matter how many fuck-ups are encountered, it's important to persist despite the fuck-ups. Consider the process like hopscotching from one fuck-up to another, but in a good way. And sometimes, this commitment to hopscotch is a day-to-day, or even moment-to-moment, practice.

Creating success is a dance where you start with the end in mind and boogie one move, even one step at a time. Sometimes the steps are slow; sometimes they are quick. In some cases, steps go backward or pause. Don't forget two steps forward and one step back is a cha-cha. Entrepreneurship is really about creating and maintaining a dance-like momentum, knowing and accepting that there will be fits and starts and refinement all along the way.

In a 2011 guest column for *Wired* magazine, innovator and founder of the $9.8 billion[1] vacuum empire, James Dyson, talked about his dances with failure, stating, "It took 5,127 prototypes and 15 years to get [my vacuums] right. And, even then, there was more work to be done. My first vacuum, DC01, went to market in 1993. We're up to DC35 now, having improved with each iteration."[2] And that was 10 years ago. Imagine the number of iterations—the trials and errors—it's taken to develop all the merchandise in their expanded product line now while still remaining the leading manufacturer of household vacuums.

Innovators and entrepreneurs like Dyson aren't afraid to try new things and they never stop after a failure. Not everything they try will work. In fact, most entrepreneurs fail multiple times before "making it," just as Dyson did. And you know what? Even after entrepreneurs "make it," they aren't immune to failure. In fact, in 2019 Dyson pulled their work in the automotive space, noting,

*The Dyson Automotive team have developed a fantastic car; they have been ingenious in their approach while remaining faithful to our philosophies. However, though we have tried very hard throughout the development process, we simply cannot make it commercially viable...I wanted you to hear directly from me that the Dyson Board has therefore taken the very difficult decision to propose the closure of our automotive project.*[3]

In the automotive update on the Dyson website, the board goes on to note that pulling the car is not a failure of the product or the team per se, but a matter of recognizing their expectations, their limitations, and their commitment to progress. "Since day one we have taken risks and dared to challenge the status quo with new products and technologies," the website states. "Such an approach drives progress, but has never been an easy journey—the route to success is never linear. This is not the first project which has changed direction and it will not be the last."

That's the thing about innovation, entrepreneurship, and love. They're all nonlinear processes; they're experimental and improvements are incremental. With each attempt, whether there's a success or "failure," there's a teachable moment carried forward to each next iteration or relationship. Repeated attempts, repeated innovations, and refinements help us learn to avoid future fuck-ups while also understanding that fuck-ups are a huge, necessary part of the process. We just have to learn how to fuck-up *better*.

*"You've got to dig in.*
*When there's an issue in the code,*
*we dig in, we understand the root cause.*
*We take the time to troubleshoot and debug.*
*You've got to do the same thing with people*
*in leadership, right? You've got to dig in.*
*And by the way, it shows people that you care."*
—EMAD GEORGY

# CHAPTER FOURTEEN

## USING DATA FOR THE GREATEST REWARDS

In the *Simple Leadership* podcast, I heard the above quote from Emad Georgy about digging in. Then, light bulbs started going on in my head, my heart, and further south; I was instantly aroused. That's the way the best business ideas work for me. They quite literally excite me. They propel me and help me connect the dots and form a greater awareness of contrasting ideas coming together. All the synapses in my brain were firing with the idea that data geeks make the best lovers. Why? Because they're always searching for the "sweet spot." I have no idea if Emad Georgy is a great lover, but it's evident from his podcast interview that he's a data geek. Hell, he's a Chief Technology Officer and owns a consultancy firm. When I listened to the interview, I became even more certain that I was onto something and decided to do a write-up on this juicy idea of data geeks' "sweet spot."

As we discussed in the last chapter, improvement is a continual practice. Failures and fuck-ups are part of the process. There's one thing about fuck-ups. They feel better when you're not alone. Regardless of innovation occurring in the bedroom or the boardroom, good partners will challenge you to go further than you might've gone alone. As a coach and editor, one of my greatest strengths is helping others achieve their highest potential. I rarely encourage clients to do the simple thing. Instead, I urge them to go after the big dreams that keep them awake at night. And when there's one step forward and two steps back in their dance, I'm there to support and encourage them to keep fucking dancing. I also make it a point to surround myself with people who do the same for me, who challenge me, and are direct with me. Even when it means they call me out on my bullshit and force me to look at innovative ways to personally improve.

As you may have guessed from my interest in data geeks, my favorite challenges are both collaborative and sexy. It may sound like an odd combination, but it's not. I love the way Vishen Lakhiani's book, *The Buddha and the Badass,* introduces the concept of "idea sex." "Idea sex is when two thinkers come together with separate ideas and meld them together to form one new superior idea." Idea sex is brainstorming for the innovators and collaborators, and even lovers of today.

Idea sex sounds like the perfect place to cultivate the process of gathering, evaluating, and acting on data to create different realities. Peter Druker, commonly known as the father of management theories and principles, stated, "If you can't measure it, you can't improve it." Some, like Emad Georgy, the CTO who spurred this chapter, not only consider data a honing device to determine a baseline, they understand how intimate data can be. In the podcast, Georgy stated, "Metrics are my love language. It's like, Okay, so what metrics are at least showing me the reality of what's going on?"

Once we know what's happening in truth, as we have the data to see the current reality, we can start testing new approaches to get more of the results we're looking for and reduce the results we don't care for. In short, if we properly track and analyze, the right data can lead us to greater effectiveness, new innovations, and reduced costs. Whether the baseline of data shows a success, a blip, or a potential fuck-up, continuing to test and try new ideas is important to improve upon business and relationship successes. No matter how good things get, the best entrepreneurs use massive amounts of data to up the ante and achieve incremental refinement of their offers, conversions, and connections.

Growing up working in direct mail, I've always been a data geek. Long before the internet, and even before email marketing, personalized sales offers were managed most effectively through the US Postal Service. Yes, really. Back in the day, I worked with direct mail acquisition teams who'd get downright scientific in their approach to sales and marketing. No matter how great the response was to a particular direct mail package, the team worked tirelessly to continue making incremental improvements. There was always something to be tweaked in order to get a better response. Maybe they'd change the color of the envelope, add new teaser copy, or upgrade the membership card. Like direct mail, any efforts made will continue to improve with focused attention. While control and version testing strategies have evolved online with media, email, and internet ads, the basis is still the same. In our entrepreneurial worlds, continuous improvement is the name of the game and the sweet spot gets sweeter with every incremental win.

In today's world, everything can be measured. When I decided to get serious about improving my sleep patterns and physical endurance, I bought a Fitbit. Seeing my health data in black and white offered me a baseline. In data speak, the Fitbit showed me the reality of what was going on with my body. From this baseline, the progress-tracking, reminders, and education helped me make gradual and continuous improvements in several areas of my health. Seeing and meeting my daily goals quickly became a private love language for me; one where I could watch my overall health status improve, one category and one day at a time.

Remember my friend Beth Derrick's story about meeting her perfect match and getting married? Not surprisingly, Beth and her wife, Tosca, are into continuous improvements as individuals and as a married couple. In Beth's own words, here's a little tool they use on the relationship front to keep searching for the sweet spot and making it sweeter:

*At the end of each day, once our precious son and doggies are put to bed for the night, we lay in bed talking, laughing, and scheming about what we want our life to look, feel, and be like. Asking this simple question: "What can I do to make your life and our relationship better?" keeps the gates of communication open with us, which are already flung quite wide and as constant as the sunrise.*

*Being open to having this conversation in a raw and welcoming state of mind takes humility, honesty, and immense trust. The answers range from trivial to monumental, like doing laundry on a different day, or buying our first home together. It could be speculated that since we are a lesbian couple, many of the challenges of a heterosexual relationship do not exist. And while I do agree on a surface level, the love we have for each other as people permeates anything that could be an otherwise socially-defined block or challenge for us.*

*Tosca and I created a safe space within our relationship very early on, and providing that space to communicate openly with the person you share your life with is immeasurably invaluable, incomparable to anything else in life. It has been the very foundation of everything amazing that we have achieved together thus far. Every aspect of our lives has been on an upward trajectory from the moment we met. The person you choose to marry can make or break your dreams; marry the person who will make them.*

*During our nightly ritual, there's no answer that is off-limits, as this level and frequency of conversation about us stokes an innate sense of intimacy...I have to be quite frank here, having conversations like this is not something I experienced in any other relationship. It's something we've developed ourselves, because we both know how it feels to be in frustrating, unhealthy, and uncommunicative relationships. The cost of stagnation of our own personal growth, as well as the marriage's, is infinitely higher than the minimal cost of making regular, incremental or substantial changes.*

I love that so much!! Watching the relationship between Beth and Tosca evolve has been such an inspiration to me. I want to implement their process into both my intimate *and* business relationships. In romantic relationships, we often try to meet another person's needs with ease and effortlessness. We really try to make everything run smoother, create better results and greater satisfaction. However, if we don't talk about the reality of what's going on in the relationship and don't make any attempts to understand our partner's reality, there's no way we can make our intended improvements. This is true in business and intimacy. We certainly demonstrated the beauty of communication, understanding, and new processes with our Business Integration Team (BIT) mentioned in Chapter 6. Before we could experience new and improved solutions, we had to ask the hard questions and be ready to deal with the answers we received—even when the answers were "messy" and created more work. Like Beth and Tosca's relationship, addressing the messes and chaos in our business relationships is impor-tant because the value of our company's growth and profitability is infinitely higher than the minimal cost to make incremental and substantial changes to it.

Here's something important about communication, data, and the way it can upgrade our entrepreneurial experience: in order to make good decisions and encourage incremental improvements, our data must be accurate. I can't imagine our Business Integration Team communica-tion circles or Beth and Tosca's nightly conversations offering a lot of value without honesty.

Recently, I went through a rough period of insomnia when I was having difficulty falling and staying asleep. It was frustrating to no end. Each morning when I'd wake up, I'd check my sleep tracking. No matter how rested I felt, or how well I thought I'd slept, I was incred-ibly disappointed to find out my sleep time was frequently less than three hours. It's really hard to function on that little rest. I engaged additional resources to help my sleep experience, including trying new supplements and reaching out to a new health coach. After a few months without consistent progress, I started using a different sleep tracker to compare my current results. Guess what? The data my Fitbit was reporting was completely bogus. I was actually sleeping much better than the Fitbit stats recorded. Sadly, I was also trusting the data of an external source rather than the own wisdom of my own body and making decisions about my sleep experience based on that information. I'm not sure how or why it was inaccurate, but this was good news, of course. Also, it was frustrating that I made decisions based on poor data.

Let's get more detailed in what having honest data means for intimacy: I'll be the first to admit I've faked an orgasm. In all honesty, I've faked an orgasm many more times than I've enjoyed one. How helpful is that for my lovers and our sexual relationship? It isn't. A lover may get a quick ego boost while I'm left sexually-frustrated and devoid of enjoyment. Presuming a lover cares about data and wants me to experience the most amount of pleasure available, me faking an orgasm is a huge cockblock. Why? It's the furthest thing from using data as a love language because it eliminates their access to accurate data and takes away the opportunity to make incremental improvements that feel good.

We measure the things that matter because we're always looking to achieve the greatest experience. No matter how good things get, we're never truly "satisfied" because we know there's always room for improvement. That's precisely why I bought a vibrator that measures orgasmic response. Now that I can measure it, I can improve it. Sign me up for the greatest orgasmic experience—whether that's with a partner or not!

*"Love makes us wake up in the morning with a sense of purpose and a flow of creative ideas. Love floods our nervous system with positive energy, making us far more attractive to prospective employers, clients, and creative partners. Love fills us with powerful charisma, enabling us to produce new ideas and new projects, even within circumstances that seem to be limited. Love leads us to atone for our errors and clean up the mess when we've made mistakes. Love leads us to act with impeccability, integrity, and excellence. Love leads us to serve, to forgive, and to hope. Those things are the opposite of a poverty consciousness; they're the stuff of spiritual wealth creation."*
—MARIANNE WILLIAMSON

# CHAPTER FIFTEEN

## LOVE AND INDEPENDENCE

In July of 2017, after selling the Iowa home I owned for nearly 20 years, I moved to Southern California. I had a whopping $7,000 in cash, one client contract with a $1,500 monthly stipend, and the contents of my SUV. I had no idea where I'd live or what I'd do to make ends meet, but I didn't doubt that I'd be able to create the life I desired. I was on a mission and deeply in *love*—even though there was no significant other in the picture. I loved *me*, the person I was becoming, and the life I was building. I trusted the Universe to show up for me. I woke with purpose every morning. I magnetized friends, lovers, and clients. I was filled with inspiration and my mind bubbled over with new ideas that I quickly implemented. I created solutions in situations that seemed bleak. I spoke with truth and integrity. I produced amazing work.

I did all of these things effortlessly…for a while.

My hard work paid off. I crushed the six-figure mark the following year, in 2018. In 2019, I delivered my first TEDx Talk, "The Dance of Collaboration." It received rave reviews and I was hired on the spot as a keynote speaker for a women's retreat. In early 2020, I published my first book, *TranscenDANCE: Letting the Universe Lead.* It was a dream come true to finally publish the book that had been on my heart for years. Readers loved it too, submitting only five-star reviews!

As my income, influence, and outward success grew, the personal love and inspiration that once propelled me quickly diminished. I grew despondent and fell back into depressive and codependent patterns. I had the mentality that, no matter what I did in terms of accomplishments or earning, it would never be enough. Although I was making and saving more money than I'd ever had in my life, I didn't appreciate it or give myself credit for creating a business from scratch, alone, in a brand-new culture and location. I intently focused on how far I had to go rather than how far I'd actually come. This is mostly because I have such a large vision. I knew that what I'd created so far, however grand, was simply a tiny fraction of what I'm here to accomplish and achieve. I was constantly future-tripping without recognizing how good things were in the present moment. I had very little gratitude and respect for the sheer amount of success that I built and the goodness still available to me. In fact, I barely acknowledged it and often shunned it as not enough.

This negativity wasn't just a pattern associated with my entrepreneurial work, it showed up in my personal life, too. With relationships, I was always focusing on the big picture and the end result I desired— marriage—rather than enjoying each date, each lover, and each moment along the way of the journey.

The results of this pattern were soul-crushing. In my career choices, I would experience significant burnout and crash every time I'd win big with projects, assignments, or clients. Even in my corporate career, I'd be so focused on a project, I'd show almost Herculean strength in creating the best results, and then promptly get sick, and feel let down, as soon as the project was completed. In my relationships, I would self-sabotage and repeat trauma patterns each time there was a possibility of becoming close to a new lover. As a result, each budding relationship would burn out before it even got off the ground.

As much as I desired success in business and in love, I was terrified of it. I also secretly wondered if it was even possible to have both business and relationship success at the same time. I pondered if the two types of success were mutually-exclusive. On top of my mental masturbation and doubt, I hadn't figured out a way to maintain the financial gains I'd accumulated. It was as if there was a ceiling to the amount of personal happiness and personal wealth I could create and accumulate. It was like I was always waiting for the other shoe to drop, to be "found out" as imperfect, incapable, and ineffective compared to the person I purported to be. Worse, I wasn't sure I was deserving of such happiness and wealth.

I wasn't sure why this imposter syndrome plagued me, but another woman's story gave me a clue. Back in the day, when magazines were a thing, I had multiple subscriptions and I would cut out quotes that resonated with me to use on my personal vision boards. I have thousands of tiny magazine scraps with sentences and paragraphs stored. This particular quote sums up my experience of money and love. (I was unable to track the original author.)

> *She had been living above her means, splurging with money she didn't have. Why? Now she knows: "I remember, as a little kid, getting up the courage to ask my mom for money for a special school trip, and her looking at me like, 'What planet are you on? We can't afford that!'...I decided that I don't have the right to ask for what I want." It's as if all her spending as an adult—what she figured would make her "happy"—was an effort to change the painful reality that as a child she couldn't get what she wanted.*

The above sums up my experience when I asked for what I wanted as a child, or even thought about having more of something. Because of this, I came to understand that I couldn't get what I wanted, and I am the only one who can provide for my own needs, negating love and elevating independence. To date, I haven't found one person, be it parent, spouse, employer, coach, or lover who effectively supported me in finding, growing, and keeping love or money. And happiness? As hard as I tried, I hadn't found happiness in love or money.

Every time I achieved a greater level of monetary abundance, I'd be knocked back down, sometimes with a vengeance. Each time I'd topple, I went further down. I went so far down; I wasn't sure I'd even survive. I was stuck in a traumatic scheme. In 2020, my income went from the highest I'd ever earned, to lower than the annual salary I earned as a 19-year-old data entry clerk when I started in the insurance industry 30 years before. My mental health was precarious, and it was a moment-to-moment effort just to stay alive. And love? That was a shit show on repeat. Because I didn't pause dating to heal and continued to meet people while in my struggle, I connected with a series of non-committal dudes who didn't have their shit together. There's a funny thing about meeting people when you're not well. The people you meet aren't well, either. Our relationships are a mirror of our current reality. Looking back, it's no surprise I couldn't find what I wanted; I was not the person I wanted to be.

Only in retrospect, can I see several major undercurrents happening in the background of this leap-and-retreat pattern I'd been running since I moved to California. I would get shit done and accomplish great things, but I was completely unable to sustain any success I encountered. That goes for business success as well as relationship connections. I was operating solely from a masculine perspective of "making things happen" rather than leaning into my feminine and intuitive nature of "allowing things to unfold." I also started taking personal credit for the success I'd created. I stopped collaborating with team members and began taking care of everything myself. I was stuck on the "Mama 500," my son's description of the racetrack-like trauma loop I get caught in where I'm doing the same lap in my head over and over, overthinking everything. Worse, I didn't take credit, acknowledge, or invoke the Universal forces that helped to create my success in the first place.

*In other words, I fell out of love.*
*I fell out of love with myself, with others, and with God.*

The Marianne Williamson quote at the beginning of this chapter asserts the nervous system is reactive to love. To the same extent that there are positive effects of love on the nervous system, there are negative effects from the absence of love. I've found fiercely independent people, both single and partnered, often experience an absence of love and the results are detrimental. I was no exception. The evidence of love's absence in me was obvious and deep. It showed up as weight gain, insomnia, fatigue, brain fog, elevated blood pressure, incessant anxiety, binge eating, and impaired blood-glucose tolerance. Plus, pleasure of all kinds was essentially eliminated from my daily experience.

Because I lost sight of what I loved and stopped relying on others, including the support of God, I went from basking in an abundance mindset, thriving in collaboration, exchanging energy with others, and working toward a common goal, to the exact opposite. The mindset change and shift to scarcity thinking left me bone dry when it came to creativity and connectivity. In addition to love, I was most certainly missing an important element of my business and my life. I just couldn't put my finger on what it was.

Eventually, I figured it out. And it took a visit to my past and a reframe of new knowledge I'd acquired over the years to unpack it. That's up next.

*"The emotion of sex contains the secret of creative ability."*
—NAPOLEON HILL

# CHAPTER SIXTEEN

## SEX AND CREATIVITY
### WITH FEATURED AUTHOR STACEY HERRERA

In 2015, after I was let go from my corporate career and was starting my business, I ventured into a new to me territory of pleasure. As a writer and consultant where my business success was based on my personal ingenuity, I decided to examine the relationship between my sexual energy and creativity. Because I was personally going through a period I called my "Brilliant Transformation," everything in my life was changing and my sexuality was a growing part of that expansion. Professionally, I'd gone from 25 years in corporate life with the patriarchy determining my schedule and doling out my benefits to being completely in charge of my own time, my earnings, and my benefits. Personally, I'd gone from being saddled with crippling depression, people-pleasing, and stuck in bed for seven years, to enjoying my life, speaking my truth, and dancing every change I got. Sexually, I went from being single for decades and having nothing but a string of one-night stands to being in a committed and nurturing relationship.

Because I was committed to my partner and my own growth, I went to extensive lengths to heal my personal trauma, shame, and hang-ups related to sex. This exploration included hiring a sexologist and others for personal coaching, reading extensively, and receiving hands-on healing modalities like yoni (vaginal) massage. I searched far and wide in pursuit of sexual healing so I could be more effective in both my life and my business. By exploring my spirituality, I began to understand that my sacral chakra was the center of my sexuality *and* creativity; so, I understood stimulating that chakra would provide a two-fold benefit. I worked diligently to get to the place where I could fully enjoy sex and utilize it to help fuel my creative endeavors. And damn, it was enlightening and fun—especially while in a committed relationship with a sexually-open partner.

One of the biggest components of my pursuit to heal in this way was confronting a long-standing issue related to the ability to take in or receive gifts, of any kind—literal, sexual, or spiritual. As a woman, a mother, and a caretaker, I was trained to give and give and give some more. I had no idea how to receive care, attention, or even love from others. I had no training in the importance of taking time to replenish my mind, body, and soul. Since sex was never discussed in my home, and often shamed when I was growing up, there was no education on how to experience the amazing benefits that arise from sexual endeavors—namely pleasure, connection, and intimacy.

That's where featured author Stacey Herrera comes in. She and I met in 2016 when I was vigorously exploring sexuality and healing my sexual challenges. I enrolled in her Sensuality Project, a nine-month study where we had "shame-free conversations about subjects that should be shameless, because after all, life is sexually-transmitted!" Stacey was one of the main innovators contributing to my sexual healing and growth back then. She opened my mind and heart in so many ways. She was the first person to introduce masculine and feminine dynamics to me. She also cultivated a sense of the power of the present moment in me, which, like gender dynamics, was integral to sexual and career-minded success.

Because she's someone I trust and admire, and is a sought-after rela-tionship and intimacy coach, I asked her to share her views on the power of sex in business and what it looks like to be a well-fucked entrepreneur. This is what she had to say:

*I gave birth to my business in the autumn of 2012, after a long and arduous labor. At the time, I had no idea what I was getting myself into—much like the first time I had sex.*

*Business and sex are a lot alike. They both require desire, patience, and acquired skill to be successful. More importantly, to have a thriving business or a great sex life, you must be open to receive via an exchange of currency.*

*Money is often the preferred currency in business. And when it comes to sex, pleasure is the legal tender.*

*Another way to think about this would be to say, whether you want to build an empire or be a connoisseur of sensual delights, you must be willing to give and receive—wholly and completely.*

*Of course, I learned this the hard way, personally and professionally. But you don't have to because there is a fool-proof way to both add to your bottom line and guarantee your sexual pleasure—and that's <u>intimacy.</u>*

*To put it another way, profitable businesses and great sex demand your full attention, and your deliberate and active participation.*

*I had decent sex for many years—the kind of sex where orgasms were sometimes about pleasure. But more often than not, orgasm was merely the result of physical stimulation. That's the kind of sex I was having when I started my business.*

*Was I having sex regularly? Yes, sometimes in copious amounts. And while sexual energy and creative energy are the same, having a lot of sex was not making me more creative. And it most certainly was not putting more zeroes in my bank account.*

*The disconnect in my sex life was causing a disconnect in my business. And when my sex life changed for the better, my business became more profitable.*

*Of course, it took me years to make the connection.*

*As a young woman, I had grown accustomed to settling for less than I desired and deserved in my relationships. I attracted emotionally-unavailable partners who <u>performed</u> sex rather than partaking of it. My body could have easily been swapped out for any Lisa, Tina, or Jane.*

*These were not the kind of relationships I wanted. But they were the ones I was saying "Yes" to. Of course, this was not the experience my partners were having. I have a number of lovers in my wake whose lives changed for the better while we were together. And they'd happily provide testimonials to rave about the impact I had on their lives.*

*Now you might be wondering why I was not flourishing while my partners were thriving. Well, the answer is simple—there was no exchange. They took without offering because I allowed it, and I gave without asking.*

*In the summer of 2017, I made a conscious decision to live and love differently. Rather than searching for like-minded suitors, I set the intention to date like-hearted people. Because what I was longing for, more than love and more than sex, was intimacy.*

*Intimacy is what we are all longing for.*

*We want to do business with people and companies that make us feel like we matter. And sex is undeniably better when there is a connection.*

*After making this declaration, the change was almost instant.*

*A few weeks later, I went on a date with a wonderful gentleman. He was pleasant and kind, with impeccable taste in food, literature, and art. Like me, he was an insatiable bibliophile. And as I would find out later—he was great in bed.*

*Our first sexual experience lasted four glorious hours. He worshipped my body from head to toe. And he received as generously as he gave. It was a playful and intensely sensual experience. We talked like old friends and fucked like long-time lovers. It was as if we had known each other in another life.*

*That was the first of my many well-fucked experiences.*

*You see, everything in the Universe operates on the barter-and-trade system. And because life in and of itself is all about creation, it makes sense that sexual energy is a highly profitable currency.*

*Well-fucked people know this.*

*People who have more sex tend to be happier and have higher self-esteem, which, in turn, makes them more attractive to potential clients and customers. That explains why people who have more sex make more money.*

*But here's the rub: the amount of money we generate and the amount of sex we have are in direct proportion to our ability to give and receive—the exchange of currency.*

*As to the question of quality versus quantity, well, you already know the answer to that. Quality tops quantity all day, every day.*

*Quality sex necessitates intimacy.*

*It's nearly impossible to have a fulfilling life, build a prosperous business, or reach our full erotic potential without the richness of intimacy.*

*Intimacy is a biological need.*

*The need for physical and emotional closeness is hardwired into our humanity. Touch is the only sense that we cannot live without, and our emotions color the experiences of our lives.*

*The desire to be physically held and emotionally naked is innate. But so often, we are either unaware of the desire or are afraid to express it. This explains why sex is not always intimate.*

*Sometimes sex is just sex. And using sex as a substitute for intimacy will leave your heart empty and your bank account overdrawn.*

*But when sex and intimacy come together (pun intended)—magic happens. It's what I like to call being well-fucked.*

*The well-fucked entrepreneur knows that pleasure yields an unlimited return. They prioritize intimacy in their sexual experiences because it puts them in the receptive mode.*

*The well-fucked entrepreneur is not interested in putting a stranglehold on their desires because they know exactly how they want to feel. And they know that surrender is the fastest route to fulfillment.*

*The well-fucked entrepreneur knows that pleasure and power are two sides of the same coin. Because you cannot have one without the other—and together they make it rain.*

*Money and sex come from the same well. And when you are sexually empowered, people trust you. They want to hire you and support your vision.*

*To sum it up, the more intimacy-fueled sex you have, the easier it is to build your empire. And as you become more and more uninhibited, sexually-speaking, the more (fill in the blank with your most seductive desire) you can have.*

A lack of intimacy—particularly in the wake of a global pandemic—most certainly was a contributing factor to the slump I was experiencing in my life and my business. I was the furthest from being well-fucked that I'd been since I started my entrepreneurial journey—and it showed. This made me curious about the couples who build businesses together. I wondered "what do they know that I don't?" Next, I got really curious about how they balance having both a business and a relationship.

*"Be a boss. Date a boss.*
*Build an empire."*
—UNKNOWN

# CHAPTER SEVENTEEN

## WHEN BUSINESS AND INTIMACY UNITE
### WITH FEATURED AUTHOR MARTA WILDE

As synchronicity would have it, my ailing physical and emotional health, coupled with the insomnia and weight-gain I experienced in 2020 put me smack in front of Cliff and Marta Wilde's health coaching services. From my first meeting with Cliff, I could tell he was a data geek. He's constantly nose-deep in health research and works hard to make connections, and help clients get to the root of their problem. He uses a simplified and systematic approach to get to a resolution to the stickiest of problems. At the time, I was suffering from the worst bout of brain fog I'd ever had and was sleeping only a few hours each night. Before my first meeting with Cliff, I completed a detailed question-naire addressing my health from several angles. Some of the questions caught me totally off guard, like, "Do you get tired after eating carbs or gluten?" I had no idea, but the question alone helped me make connections I hadn't previously considered. I'd been operating on autopilot so long, I had no idea the havoc my irregular meal schedule and food choices were wreaking on my life. One of the things Cliff said on the call caused me to tear up. In response to my weight gain, he said, "Your body is actually protecting you. It's doing exactly what it's designed to do." I'm not sure why that hit me so hard, but it did. I spent so much time hating on my body for being larger and not functioning as efficiently as I'd like. However, I'd never once considered how beautifully designed it is and how fortunate I am that it automatically signals my own misalignment through illness. This wasn't the first time dis-ease caused an awakening in me. I'd suffered some pretty hasty notices from my body in the form of dis-ease and chronic illness. However, in the past, I generally failed to heed my body's notice and take appropriate action before it was too late and my body was literally screaming at me. Even with my body's legitimate cries for attention, I had no understanding of the beauty of its signals. And I sure as hell didn't appreciate the disruption dis-ease caused. Thanks to Cliff's wisdom, it was the first time I acknowledged the imbalance and had an appreciation for it.

Another breakthrough came about as we worked more closely with my diet and physical activity levels to stabilize my blood sugar, showing signs of glucose intolerance. For the prior several months, I'd been struggling to work and get anything accomplished in my business. I was basically writing everything off as "no longer aligned." In reality, I was working with some of the most aligned and supportive clients I've ever collaborated with. Work wasn't hard because it wasn't aligned; it was hard because I wasn't operating at a high level physically or emotionally. That was actually music to my ears, because it reminded me that my physical and emotional health is completely within my control.

While Cliff manages the physical aspects of health for clients, his wife Marta is the perfect complement who addresses the emotional aspects of one's health. She's focused on mindset, breathwork, hypnosis, and retraining the nervous system to accommodate and support lasting health changes.

After experiencing the yin and yang of their work first-hand, I reached out and asked them to share their experience of uniting business and intimacy. This is what Marta had to say:

*I still remember arriving at London's Victoria Coach Station with two bags, £300 (about $425) in my pocket, and a then on-and-off boyfriend in tow. I now understand that his presence was to lend me a false sense of security, as I deep down didn't trust myself to do this on my own. Of course, this is a very different scenario than actually connecting with your soul mate to fulfil your life's purpose.*

*That was back in 2004. I left Poland, my home country, with high hopes and quite unclear dreams of something better.*

*What was this better thing? And what was it better than? I am not sure if even today, 17 years later, I'd be able to give you a clear answer.*

*Cliff was at university at the time, but he was a mess, drinking himself into oblivion, weighing two stones heavier (14 kg or 28 pounds) than he does now, struggling with a nasty autoimmune disease, and popping pills as the docs said that was his only option. Like me at the time, he was equally clueless as to what he wanted to do with his life.*

*Fast forward to early 2009 with me in corporate recruitment (having had several jobs since arriving in London that summer afternoon in August 2004), Cliff in corporate finance.*

*We didn't know each other at that point, yet both decided to leave the corporate hamster wheel and pursue a career change in fitness. And in spring 2009, with some clearly Divine intervention, we ended up taking the same personal training course.*

*The course, apart from the usual fitness work, was also heavily focused on teaching nutrition. And not the kinda stuff that your doctors tell you. The course was the real thing!*

*Even though we were in separate study groups, a shared drink at a pub got us hooked and infatuated quickly with each other, though neither of us wanted to admit it at the time. Here we are, 12 years later sharing our story with you.*

*Very quickly into our new careers, initially working in separate jobs, we figured out that there's sooooo much more to fitness, nutrition, and health! We understood there was so much more we could help our clients with.*

*In 2011 after continuing our education and diving much deeper into nutrition and nutritional therapy rather than just fitness, circumstances aligned for both of us to start our self-employed businesses. Separate at first, yet joining forces within a few weeks of making that leap, we felt like we could do so much more of this work together—and do it better.*

*Within months we were not just super busy with clients (most of them followed us once we left our previous jobs and new ones joined through recommendations quickly) but also considering opening our own facility.*

*Yet something wasn't sitting quite right with me...*

*I told Cliff how much I always wanted to travel and I didn't want to regret that in five years when I felt tied down by our premises and brick-and-mortar business. Yet, I must mention that vagabonding and nomad entrepreneurship was a complete taboo for us both at the time.*

*Cliff agreed, and within weeks—to the grand confusion and disbelief of our family, friends, and clients—we packed everything and set off backpacking around the world for almost a year. Amongst a few sleepless nights, very limited budget and about a million sand fly bites—it was blissful!*

*We got engaged at sunrise on Christmas Day on Koh Chang in Thailand and after our South East Asian adventures, we ended up renting the smallest and cheapest campervan for six weeks, cruising down the east coast of Australia.*

*A few months later, after crisscrossing the north and the south islands of New Zealand, we totally and utterly fell in love with the country and settled in Aukland for a few months.*

*After returning to the UK, attempting to start our online business, spending over a year stumbling along in the dark with a blindfold on, trying to pin the tail on the donkey, we happened to meet our very first mentors through an event our friend invited us to.*

*That was October 2013. In six short weeks, we not only made back our investment in working with them (that fully went on a credit card I must note here), but actually earned quite a significant amount of extra cash in addition.*

*It was exciting, exhilarating, and frankly speaking, quite unbelievable. With some fairly basic marketing advice and a total mindset transformation (and this was key—without that shift we would have gone nowhere), we were not only helping people in the way we always wanted, but also making a decent living in return and bringing in in just the first two or three months of 2014 what we initially believed we could maybe, just maybe, bring in in the entire year!*

*We've always been known for fast action when something resonates with us. Tell us what to do and if it feels good, we'll do it. That was our motto throughout the 18 months of the work we did with our mentors.*

*We got married in between in June 2014 and joined our mentors' retreat with a mini honeymoon on the beautiful Mediterranean island of Cyprus.*

*Within a few months, we called Cyprus our home as we've always wanted to make the move and leave the UK for far warmer and sunnier climates. Yet we weren't sure when and where.*

*Then it happened!*

*And I know what you're thinking right now.*

*It all sounds so simple and easy and just oh so idyllic.*

*Yet was it fuck!*

*Enter stage left...the entrepreneurial success hangover!*

*Between 2014 and 2017 we kept growing and growing, both personally and in the business. We were growing educationally, deepening our knowledge, growing emotionally, learning (often the hard way) to hold our growth and success and growing spiritually, exploring the vast unknown of the seemingly intangible world that we somehow knew was driving us strongly.*

*As amazing as it was to be living in this sunny paradise in a house that previously we've only ever dreamed of, the challenges of getting to know each other deeper and deeper as a husband and wife on all levels and learning how the hell to run this thing that was supposed to be our business was, for years a rather bumpy ride.*

*With Cliff unable to fully and openly communicate his emotions (hello, toxic modern perception of masculine), shutting down and retreating inwards whenever there was a perceived challenge.*

*And me...well, the Eastern European firecracker with some serious emotional baggage, I used to scream and shout and break things, often end up with panic attacks, swinging in and out of depression. Because I didn't feel safe within myself, I couldn't allow myself to trust anyone fully (regardless of how loving and supportive they were towards me), and I felt like I was in it all on my own (that's the modern hurt and scared feminine for you).*

*I don't know how much you know and explore the concepts of masculine and feminine energy in your own life. Yet for us, understanding polarity was inherently one of the most important parts of our journey.*

*And again, these concepts were helpful both as a couple and business partners.*

*Allowing the energies to dance and play and trusting that leaning in to our intuition was often key here.*

*The forever shifting and changing like in a kaleidoscope business and romance dynamic…*

*On one side those two get to stay separate, yet on the other, they forever blend and penetrate every waking moment (and sometimes even our dreams) as they're so inseparable.*

*We've never really argued much over the years. What happens chez Wilde is more of a heated discussion. And for years these were much more of heated monologues courtesy of yours truly.*

*And once more, through the work we did with countless guides and mentors, we've learnt so much about creating healthy boundaries, and to know where our own respective energy fields start and where they finish. When and how they interact, blend and meld together, whether that's romantically or in the business.*

*We had to at points write out solid sets of rules as to when there's time for husband and wife life and when we are being business partners.*

*There's nothing worse than drifting off to sleep when the other says…*

*"Babe, did you remember to do this or that? Or speak about this to that client?"*

*I mean… really?*

*Yup, that used to be pretty normal!*

*Then learning to communicate consciously and openly was a process. Holy shit was that a humongous journey. Practicing speaking to each other about our deepest feelings and sharing our frustrations without blaming and pointing a finger was interesting. One thing that really stuck out to me that was said by one of our mentors was "when you're pointing a finger at someone, there are three fingers pointing right back at you."*

*So yes…we had to learn hard how to stop playing the victim!*

*We're both strong believers it is not the circumstance but our attitude that dictates the outcome.*

*Over the years, we left the fitness world behind and grew and expanded to where we are today with our life and our business. We've become what some people describe as "The Health Fixers," doing things no one else could, bringing the deepest aspects of human physiology, emotions, and minds together for greater health and happiness.*

*Yet that wasn't without turbulence…*

*2018 (individually and together) was likely one of the hardest years of our lives, and knowing that my dad passed away in 2017 and Cliff was diagnosed with a brain tumour when he was only 17 is saying something…*

*Through the depths of challenges, identity crises, and emotional struggle between 2018 and 2019 we've learnt so, so much!*

*Once again dropping a quote here: "the gift is always in the shit!" And boy was this turd wrapped up in a glittery and sparkly wrapper!*

*Accepting just how paradoxical our life on planet Earth is and learning to roll with the concept of duality was key!*

*Knowing when to pause and pull away to take a deep breath and reassess and when to confidently charge forward while honouring the forever changing seasons in our romance and business.*

*And most of it came from our (built over the years) strong resilience and relentless work on ourselves and the relationship with each other.*

*Since we first met in 2009, we've lived together in four countries, and moved I can't even remember how many times. There were times when we couldn't stand or handle each other, thinking that the only way out is a divorce to then fall in love once again even harder. We went sexless for weeks, if not months at a time, as our polarity was non-existent to then discover yet another depth of our physical and spiritual connection and explore our bodies, energies, and minds even deeper. At one point spent 18 months in a polyamorous relationship that allowed us both to access the deepest and most vulnerable parts of ourselves while learning to communicate even more openly. Started and burnt down several business ideas. Hired and fired numerous team members. Got in debt and got out of it. Spent money we didn't have and learnt to save and invest wisely. Travelled the world, got the cutest rescue dog who's now been with us for five years as our little baby. Helped hundreds of people from 25+ countries across this globe that we all call home. Learnt stuff we deeply cherish and trust and also embarked on some pretty useless (to us) learning journeys, simply thinking we needed to know this or that.*

*And all that maneuvering and balancing this act of doing business and life together sometimes feeling like we're not just twin flames but in fact a split soul and sometimes feeling like we've come from two separate worlds that just can't communicate with and understand each other.*

*So yeah... it hasn't always been easy!*

*Yet, when you know that you have a common goal and you know that easy or hard is a choice and simply just a perception. You do the work as there simply just isn't another option. And as we often tell our friends and laugh hard about it—we're unemployable and not having a Plan B has certainly been the driving force and a blessing in disguise as we just keep going.*

*No matter what, over the years, several people, countless times said this one thing to us, in pretty much the same words:*

*"You are still together and still here because you can handle each other!"*

*A few years ago, we wrote the 12 Unlimited Life Attributes (a set of commandments of sorts) that I want to share with you as truly from the bottom of our hearts. Whether consciously or not, over the years, these commandments have been our life savers!!*

*Living my unlimited life, I:*

*1. always speak everything I think*

*2. communicate clearly and specifically*

*3. remain conscious and do not cower nor attack great/strong energies*

*4. nourish my body with food choices that serve me, with no guilt, shame, or emotional attachment*

*5. move with ease and flow choosing movement and activity I enjoy and that serves me*

*6. always follow my excitement to the best of my ability*

*7. surrender to greater good and let go of any attachment to any specific outcome*

*8. understand that resentment and resistance always show up for me to respond differently and step up to the next level (the only way for me to experience my shift is to respond differently to what initially looks the same)*

*9. am the creator of my experience in its entirety*

*10. see the lesson in every situation and understand there's no good or bad, no right or wrong – everything just is and everything is feedback - and only I can choose whether it serves me or not in that moment*

*11. create and live my life in abundance in all areas of my life (abundance is the ability to do what I get to do when I get to do it)*

*12. feel all emotions and feelings fully*

*"Having a giving spirit does not mean having
a spirit of self-sacrifice or martyrdom.
The martyr still sees the dualism between helping oneself
and helping others, viewing these two as being in conflict.
That's not generosity: that's just being a
card-carrying co-dependent."*
—BOB BURG AND JOHN DAVID MANN

# CHAPTER EIGHTEEN

## GIVING WITHOUT STRINGS

One of the things I learned when I really delved into my own healing was how much I value a sense of community and collaboration. I love it so much; that it was the basis of the TEDx talk I delivered in 2019. I titled my talk "The Dance of Collaboration" and even built the brand "Collaborative AF" to work in partnership with others. While I'd learned the difference between giving from a place of expecting something in return and giving generously with a pure heart—sans strings— it wasn't until after my TEDx and new brand launch that I could more clearly see my problem. It was apparent I still had underlying motives tied to my personal wounds. Granted, the knots had loosened, and they were far less obvious, but they were still present.

It was easier to see these "flaws" in other people and the way they covertly and overtly manipulated their partners and collaborators by giving with strings. Much to my surprise, a few of those people showed up in my life in 2019 to hammer this point home. One man in particular held an opportunity over my head asking me to "humble myself" because he helped me get a TEDx talk—all the while being angry and resentful that I didn't publicly acknowledge enough him for the connections and coaching he freely offered to our group. At least, I thought the connection was given freely. And the coaching? It was a group effort as we all coached one another. He also told me certain coaches charge $10,000-$50,000 to help people get TEDx talks and ended the conversation with a biting tone, stating, "I don't want anything in return but a thank you would be nice." Trust me, I did thank him. In fact, I gushed over his supposed generosity. I also told many people about how we serendipitously met and that he graciously connected me to the TEDx community.

In actuality, the offer and opportunity to speak in the same community with him wasn't free at all. There was a cost to his "kindness." The connection and coaching he offered came with unspoken expectations and an assumption that he'd benefit in some way from the work I did. Frankly, I have no problem with other people benefiting from the work that I do. That's one of the greatest benefits of collaboration. However, the benefits typically come in the form of referral agreements, and they should be addressed up front with clarity and honesty. In the end, this man and I parted ways after I relayed to him that there's nothing wrong with having expectations, but when you're not transparent about them and hold them over people's heads, it's totally uncool.

That experience and the mirror it held up to me created reflections that really brought to light some deep wounding I still needed to address. When I summarized my wins and losses for 2019 as part of my annual review process, this is what I documented about the wounding: "I launched a new business platform called Collaborative AF, to really focus on the connections I'd made with others and the way we do business together. A short month or two after launch, it was clear that most of my collaborations were one-sided; I did most of the efforting and managed the emotional labor while others received the benefits. I slowly backed away from nearly every collaboration I was involved in. I quickly realized the new platform was built on trauma and a desire to fit in—often in places I don't belong."

*In other words, I was a card-carrying codependent giving from a place of martyrdom and not generosity.*

As much as it pains me to admit it, while I didn't directly confront others, I was no different from the man who shoved his help in my face. Looking back on my most significant intimate relationship with this new lens, brought everything into perspective for me. I was intimately familiar with the role codependency played in my relationships, but this was the first time it was clear to me from a business perspective. Plus, a chance encounter with a date enabled me to be on the other end of efforting and helped me get the message loud and clear.

In a 2015 romantic relationship, I immediately jumped in and took care of things like laundry, cleaning, and cooking. I also went all-out with gifting, surprises, and other acts of service. "Acts of service" is my love language, so they come naturally to me. I honestly didn't think I was doing any of these things with an expectation to get something in return, and considered the acts more of a time-management strategy. I thought if I did the housework, my boyfriend and I could spend more time together when he was off work. As a business owner, he was overly-committed to his profession and easily worked more than 50 hours each week. Early on, he told me he didn't expect me to do any extra work and he really just wanted me to "be." He told me he liked me as I was and I didn't have to "perform" or buy gifts in order to receive his love. It's not that I didn't believe him; it was more like I didn't believe that for myself. I've always felt like I had to earn everything—especially love, and even my right to exist. Because of this tendency, I fell into codependent giving as a way to accommodate for my inner wounds. Often, particularly with my parents, I gave from a place of guilt, shame, and a huge desire to be validated. As the youngest child of parents who weren't really interested in parenting or being involved in my life, giving and performing became a way to get attention—and sometimes a bit of love in return. I'm not sure I ever saw a proper example of what it looks like to give without strings. It seems everyone around me was keeping score and there was an expectation of a return in some way, shape, or form. This made receiving gifts or thanks extra difficult because the tab was constantly running, racking up debts—if only in my own mind. While receiving sounds amazing in theory—as a codependent, it's sometimes more challenging for me. At least with giving, I'm in control and don't have to give when I choose not to. I have very little conscious control over receiving and because my brain is constantly calculating the "debt," I constantly feel like I'm behind the 8-ball instead of being on even ground with the giver.

The problem in my relationship with my boyfriend was that when I did the acts of service, I did them at my own prompting, not because of an agreement we made. There was no invitation for me to help. While I didn't think I had an ulterior motive, at least not consciously, I can now see that I wanted to be validated, loved, and chosen. The truth was my boyfriend had already chosen me. My doing the extra work, the code-pendent stuff, pushed him away more than it drew him in. Doing the housework and other chores I thought helpful were actually emascu-lating him because he hadn't led me to do them. I became resentful because he didn't appreciate the work I did. When he offered or didn't offer something in response to my actions, there's no way his energy could come from a clear place because I'd already hijacked It by taking the lead. Except, I had no idea this was going on. I did realize it, several years later, when it was much too late to salvage the relation-ship. Reading the content on sex, creativity, and intimacy from featured author Stacey Herrera hit me like a ton of bricks. When she talked about her partners thriving when she was not because of a lack of exchange, I felt that statement in my core. My understanding deepened when she recalled that she allowed her partners to take without giving because she gave without asking.

In 2020, I had a date with someone I met on a dating app. While we knew we weren't going to be in a relationship because he wanted to have kids and I'm not in the market for that, we had enough similar interests to develop a friendship. When I got back from our first meet-ing, he sent me three emails with resources, books, links, and things he thought would help me on my journey. I hadn't asked for any of it. He sent so much data, it shut down my computer. I kindly thanked him, then promptly deleted everything he'd sent. I didn't want, need, or appreciate the action he took because I didn't ask for it, nor did I have a need for the items he supplied.

One of the reasons he and I connected was because he was writing a book, and wasn't sure how to go about it. I have a stellar resource template for book writing that he wanted. At the time, I was selling it at a nominal price and I knew he could afford it. Instead of sending him the link to purchase, I sent him the resources for free. Why? Because I felt guilty; like I should offer him something of value in return for what he sent me, even though I didn't ask for or want any of the items he sent. I'm not claiming getting something for free was his motive for sending me the resources. However, what became clear to me was my response. My "gift" to him, wasn't such a gift because I gave from a place that wasn't energetically clear. In other words, it was codependent.

> *I gave out of guilt, not inspiration.*
> *That's a recipe for resentment.*

This chance interaction with a stranger from a dating app gave me a clear picture of how my ex-boyfriend years ago must've felt when I took care of his home. It gets better though. Or worse, depending on how you look at it.

Part of the resource I sent the dating app dude included a list of commonly misused words. It was about four pages of words like "effect/affect," "complement/compliment," and "whose/who's," with descriptions and instructions on how to use each in a sentence. A day or so later, he sent me a new document with my data completely reformatted. He took it upon himself to alphabetize the list of commonly misused words from my book resource.

Instead of being grateful and appreciative, like he probably expected me to be, I was insulted for two reasons. First, because I hadn't asked him to do that. Second, when I built the list, I specifically chose *not* to put them in alphabetical order. Here's why: in alphabetical order, the most common misused words like "your/you're" and "their/there/they're" would be at the end of the list instead of the beginning. In my book, that defeats the purpose.

I never spoke to him again.

I suspect the dating app dude wrote me off as an ungrateful bitch, in the same way I often considered my ex-boyfriend an ungrateful asshole. In reality, the dating app dude was behaving just as I did back in the day with my ex. After experiencing it from the opposite side of the interaction, I can see how my ex-boyfriend must've felt. I now understood that the responsibility of the energetic discomfort I experienced with my ex was mine. I chose to do tasks I wasn't specifically asked to do. Doing unnecessary work in an attempt to earn something automatically created resentment when I didn't get what I expected in return for my efforts. Author Robert Holden, Ph.D., discusses the difference between doing something to get love and giving freely in his book *Lovability.* He says, "If you give love in order to get love, you will end up feeling disappointed and resentful...When you give love freely, you feel the love you give, and you feel loveable no matter the return." In addition to the internal conflict of resentment, the lack of clarity and lack of communication put the other person in an uncomfortable place. My interaction with the dating app dude made the problem of codependent giving crystal clear for me.

In order to make my dating experiences run more smoothly, I've been studying polarity and masculine and feminine communication. According to Zak Roedde, a polarity coach and author of *Irresistibly Feminine: How to Activate a Man's Everlasting Devotion to Your Heart,* "Masculine energy actively leads to a specific outcome. Feminine energy expresses without trying to get an outcome." Feminine communication is deeply vulnerable and unattached at the same time. When addressing freedom from manipulation, Roedde goes on to say, "Feminine energy from a woman activates a man's devotion because she is energetically leaving it up to him to decide whether to lead.

Masculine energy from a woman suppresses (a man's devotion) because she's trying to get an outcome from him."

Recently, I got a chance to try this out while talking with a new date. I mentioned how important dancing—specifically partner dancing—is to me. He said, "So you're going to make me take partner lessons?" I responded, "No. I'm not asking you to do anything. I'm only saying that partner dancing is important to me." I presented my need, remained completely unattached to the outcome, and invited him to choose the response that resonated with him. This was much different than the approach I took with my ex-boyfriend, where I signed us up for dance lessons, and he tagged along begrudgingly while I attempted to lead the whole time.

My friends and I often pop off obligatory responses like my new date did because most of us are coaches. We instantly go into coaching mode when people come to us with problems. Then we wonder why we're exhausted. In reality though, most times, people aren't coming to us to be coached; they're coming to us for support. My son hit the nail on the head once when he reminded me of my tendency to coach: "Right now I need a little less life coach and a little more mama." His ability to communicate his need clearly helped me to better meet him where he was; and to lessen the emotional load I was unnecessarily carrying. Because of my tendency to coach, advise, and teach, I've been more careful about asking whoever I'm chatting with if they're looking for support or solutions before offering any advice.

Friends' and lovers' resentments about being coached seemed more pronounced in my personal relationships, but they definitely showed up in my business partnerships as well. Apparently, I wasn't alone either. A friend and agency owner vented in a Facebook group that clients expecting out-of-scope services is a form of "manipulation" that conditions business owners to perform extra services without payment. This exchange helped me understand this phenomenon of giving and feeling bitterness building—without realizing that my own giving causing the problem in the first place. Our commentary alerted me to the fact that the same codependent dynamics I'd experienced in relationships exist professionally, too, although I'd done a pretty good job of minimizing the negative impact. Here's what that looks like. Personally, I love to go above and beyond for my clients. However, I completely understand that everything I do that's outside the scope of our contract is on me. I can't do something extra for clients as a gift without asking for payment and have an expectation for them to pay. Nor can I carry resentment about choosing to do something extra and not getting recognition for it. Once I've spelled out my terms, every single thing I do that's "above and beyond" the contract is truly a gift and it needs to come from a clear energetic space in me, with an open heart and no expectation of return.

At the same time, I've experienced giving of myself in business that's win-win. Sometimes, out-of-scope requests feel right for both parties. Creating clear expectations in the form of contracts requires a bit of up-front work, but it establishes expectations, standards, and obligations for both parties from the get-go. When a contract's expectations are clear, if a client has a request that's not covered in the contract, it's decision-time for me. I can choose to take care of their request without asking for payment, knowing that it's a gift and having no ill feeling about it. Or, I can choose to create a new, separate agreement for the out-of-scope request and ask the client to pay for the new work. For me, this process has to be that cut-and-dry.

In my insurance career as a Service Delivery Manager, I gained intimate experience with the dynamics of out-of-scope projects and the drain it places on a team, especially when expectations and service levels are not managed well. The need to deliver services outside of contract terms can, in fact, feel like manipulation. And yet, there's often a deeper issue at play.

Here's an example of a deeper issue that played out in this scenario: our team was accustomed to doing everything for free to appease clients after a particularly disruptive systems conversion. As part of the new system integration, long-term clients with very detailed and specific out-of-the-box customizations were converted to standardized, almost cookie-cutter-like services. Because clients were so unhappy and even furious about the new system, we did anything and everything we could to keep client revenue on the books. This exhausting pattern drained our personnel and kept clients from seeing the benefits of the brand-new baseline for our standard services. The deeper problem was that the newly-implemented systems had bugs that kept us from delivering even our standardized services consistently. As a result, we put out fires daily and jumped through more hoops than I could count.

It took some serious dedication, overtime, and heavy lifting to shore the ship and minimize the near-constant fires. However, as soon we garnered integrity and performance levels with our basic systems and services, it was time to stand firm in our value—and that meant requiring payment for extras, customizations, and special requests. While we continued to offer some extra services for free in the name of goodwill offerings, we began to recognize extraneous bids not included in client contracts. At my direction, we started acknowledging all the "added value" services our team provided. At a minimum, we listed the "extra" services on invoices with zero cost when we chose to deliver them for free. When we billed for out-of-scope services, we charged a premium for them—without a hint of disappointment from our clients, because we'd established our baseline service level, clarified expectations, and delivered consistently. I got so good at completing out-of-scope contracts, our management team took notice, as did the other Service Delivery Managers. Suddenly, we had a new revenue stream and eliminated the feeling of being strong-armed or manipulated by our clients. Management was so impressed with the turn of events that they even created a profitability award and fat bonus for me to recognize my work initiating the most billable, out-of-scope projects.

Team members no longer felt resentful, unappreciated, and manipulated for doing "extras," and clients were satisfied knowing that both their contracted needs and their special requests were provided for—even when it meant they had to dig a little deeper into their pocketbook to pay for them. We achieved this balance through solid, documented contracts, education about the value of our services, and open, clear communication with our customers. Having those tools in place ensured the team delivered consistently, gave team members the leeway to give additional services as a gift, and set the expectation that accommodations for special needs would always be met with equal reciprocation from both parties.

Giving from the heart offers a gift to the recipient. When we give in this way, in business and in relationships, we often receive a gift, too. It's important to give without strings and without expectations. Giving with strings and expectations is a form of manipulation which doesn't feel good for either party. On the other hand, effective giving can create positivity all around. Just follow the advice of one of the most popular motivational speakers ever, Zig Ziglar, who said, "You can have everything in life you want, if you will just help other people get what they want." Business authors Bob Burg and John David Mann give instructions for this in their book *The Go-Giver*, noting "If you place the other person's interests first, *your* interests will always be taken care of. *Always.* Some people call it *enlightened self-interest.* Watch out for what other people need, with the faith that when you do, you'll always get what *you* need."

*"Try not to confuse attachment with love.*
*Attachment is about fear and dependency and has more to*
*do with love of self than love of another.*
*Love without attachment is the purest love because*
*it isn't about what others can give you because you're empty.*
*It is about what you can give others because*
*you're already full."*
—YASMIN MOGAHED

# CHAPTER NINETEEN

## DEEP CONNECTION VERSUS DEEP ATTACHMENT

For the last several years, I've been following a Facebook group for women that addresses masculine/feminine dynamics, and helps women become empowered to express their feminine radiance. Group leaders and members talk frequently about the value of having a "man funnel." In this view, a funnel is a means of not immediately attaching to a date before ensuring said man demonstrates the qualities you're looking for in a mate.

I have to confess, I've always been one to immediately attach to the men I date, often claiming exclusivity immediately—if only in my own mind. What I know now, after extensive personal and professional development work, is that my tendency to attach so quickly is both unhealthy and unwise. One of the biggest benefits of the dating funnel is that it's set up to prevent early attachment. It both lessens the likelihood of getting too serious too soon, and provides an opportunity to learn about prospects and vet them as a good match before becoming committed. Essentially, the dating funnel is a tool that facilitates due diligence; it helps ensure daters seek compatibility without unnecessarily putting blinders on right away and becoming desperately exclusive. One of my Facebook friends, Wendy Burrell, drafted a graphic that my friend Karla Singson and her agency Scalewind polished to represent how the "man funnel" works. Check out the funnel as a dating tool (note the timing and date numbers are not prescriptive but representative):

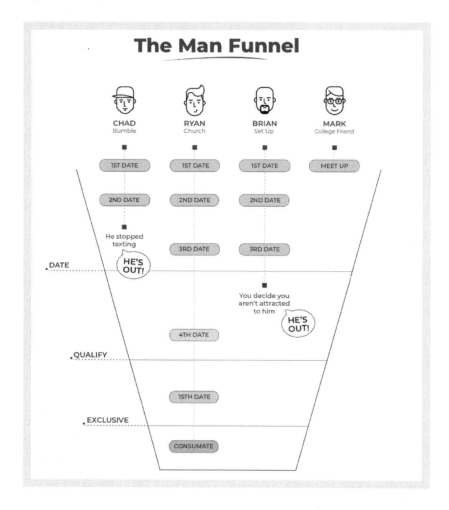

Women aren't the only ones with a funnel. One of the men I met on a dating app, Robin Treen, explained the funnel from a man's perspective on our first date. As we were talking, he mentioned that he is frequently proposed to on the first or second date. I'm not sure he meant that literally, but he went on to say, "I check off a lot of boxes

for women and they immediately want to get attached and move in."
For reference, here are the checkboxes I surmised from our conversation: emotionally-available and aware, masculine leader, successful business owner, homeowner, involved parent to his grown kids, significant time-lapse after an amicable divorce, adventurous, and undoubtedly single. He definitely checked off many of my boxes, and I can honestly say I've been guilty of attaching to a man's attributes before truly knowing him personally. I've sometimes gotten so excited to be connected with a new man that I've failed to allow his actions to speak to his level of commitment and demonstrate the truth of the attributes he claims. Actions always speak louder than any checkboxes I may've gotten starry-eyed about early on, whether or not those boxes were actually fulfilled.

I mentioned the value of dating multiple people and having a dating funnel. He replied, "People need to understand that dating is a competition. I mean, it's our first date. I don't even know your last name, nor have I had a chance to cyberstalk you and find out what you're *really* about." With his astute response, he made two things really clear to me. First, by referring to dating as a competition, it was obvious that he uses some form of a funnel for his dates too. He further solidified his use of a funnel when he said, "I don't sleep with strangers." How novel and smart. For the record, his declaration was simply conversational, not a response to the opportunity to do so. Second, he was waiting for my actions and internet history to help fill in the gaps of my story. My online presence is vast and I've written about so many personal things publicly that complete strangers could know more about me than some of my own family members. As a side note, while I appreciate it when someone takes the time to learn more about me through internet sleuthing, I did think it was cool that he chose to meet me in person first.

No matter how authentic we are, a person on a first date can't know us, and we certainly can't know them in such a short amount of time—no matter how instant, remarkable, or deep the connection feels. Particularly at our ages, having passed the half-century mark, we've built really cool lives. We have responsibilities with our children, maybe grandchildren, and commitments to entrepreneurship. Those responsibilities aren't things easily handed over to someone you just met.

I love the idea of spending time with a variety of people and getting to know them as casually or intimately as the situation calls for. I love the idea of maintaining dominion over my own life, and then choosing to connect further when it's aligned, and seeing front-runners emerge from the dating pack. When we think of a funnel from a business perspective, it's a mechanism to welcome prospects into the customer journey. There's no partiality and each prospect receives the same treatment. As we discussed in Chapter 5, success is a numbers game. A funnel begins with a higher number of prospects and ends with a much smaller number of committed and vetted clients. Most prospects are fulfilling a curiosity when they hit a landing or sales page. Some will check out the lead magnet or sign up for the mailing list. Others take it to the next level and buy an entry-level product, as a way to "kick the tires" of a business. Some will be repeat customers who traverse a company's various offers. A few will go all the way—becoming super fans and loyal advocates of a person's work, and lining up to buy every product and service while singing praises to their friends and associates.

What's the best way to create super fans and loyal advocates of your work? Essentially, be real. Be yourself and connect deeply with your clients. Be the same person in person you purport to be in your advertisements. Here's what that looks like: Have integrity, operate with transparency, and be authentic. Be consistent in your actions and deliver what you say you're going to deliver. Be honest and make amends when you screw up. One of my first clients as an entrepreneur was a media company in California. I worked directly with their CEO for three years before we met in person after I moved. When we finally met for lunch, she gave me one of my favorite compliments I've ever received, stating, "You're exactly the same person in real life as you are online or at a distance." It's true. I'm Melissa and I'm the same friend as I am business owner—

passionate, fairly demanding, occasionally strange, generally uncon-ventional, consistent with delivery, and most importantly, honest—always and in all ways. For me, having a thriving business is directly related to finding clients who see and appreciate these values so much that they become super fans. This particular CEO client was such a super fan of mine that she continued to develop new opportu-nities for me to collaborate with her and earn higher paychecks from her organization.

Creating super fans in the dating world works the same way, except so many people, including me, jump to deep attachment instead of creating a deep connection first. When a person is focused on deep attachment, they're typically doing everything they can to be "a good catch." Especially for those of us with codependency issues, this attachment includes consciously or unconsciously renouncing parts of who we are and covering up our true yearnings in order to be accepted. In essence, we're afraid to let our freak flag fly for fear it would scare off potential suitors. Dr. Nicole LePera, known as the Holistic Psychol-ogist on social media, remarks on the reason people do this, saying, "Self-betrayal is the result of conditional love—we learn to deny parts of ourselves in order to be loved not for who we are, but the version they approve of." When expecting conditional love, people do their best to make the conditions favorable for the other person to receive love. Frequently, that means daters aren't being wholly and completely themselves. The result is an attachment that's based on pretenses instead of the truth.

On the other hand, when daters show up to create deep connection, there's no fear of being too weird. And, there's no need to cover up or lie about what makes them the person they are. It's either a match or it's not—and both outcomes are ok. They trust the partnership to gradually build rather than attaching immediately to the person. They stay committed to the process of aligning with their sense of a perfect part-nership with deep connection rather than being attached to each new person they date. With this approach, when there is a match, it comes from a place of understanding and appreciating what—or rather, who

—is being offered. The connection is honest and so will last as long as it remains in integrity and alignment.

Here's the advantage I see business funnels have over dating funnels: business funnels don't get attached. I mean, how can they? Funnels are automated systems that usher prospects from one part of the sales process to another. As much as I sometimes despise the phrase, "It's business, it's not personal," it completely fits in this case. Funnels don't change their business model for anyone—and they check for alignment before progressing the connection. Entrepreneurs know nothing that happens in the funnel is personal, it's literally just business. They don't get upset if a prospect doesn't show up or drops out of their funnel. In fact, they're so busy building their business, they may not even notice. Instead of losing time grieving and rehashing purported reasons why someone deserted the customer journey, they focus on improving their process. They test conversion rates, learn from their findings, and keep at it—building and increasing connection every time they engage with prospects.

Here's another key point about business funnels. Good businesses don't invest the same amount of resources to attract and maintain customers at the top of the funnel as they do customers at the bottom of the funnel. Instead, they preserve and progressively increase resources extended to prospects—ensuring super fans who made it to the bottom of the funnel receive the most dedication and devotion.

Imagine the difference a prospective date feels when the other shows up committed to connecting through engaging conversation, versus hanging hopes on a committed future and trying to rope them into a future created in the mind. The first is engaging, and the second is manipulative. The first is also feminine and the second masculine. Whether spoken or not, dates can feel the energetic difference in people who show up for connection versus those looking for attachment. There's another advantage to connection versus attachment in dating: connection means knowing that not everyone you meet needs to become a romantic partner or lead to a relationship. Alternatively, dates could become good friends and collaborators.

This got me wondering if deep connection versus deep attachment is one of the reasons why polyamory is successful for those who participate in it. While committed polyamory focuses on deep connection and deep attachment, the idea of deep connection and low attachment is certainly the way Friends With Benefits (FWB) arrangements work. Sexual buddies who are not in a relationship often share a very deep (pun intended) connection with little to no attachment or commitment. The arrangements are not for everyone, yet they serve a purpose for those who enter them with an open mind and mutual consent.

Aside from FWB arrangements, there are business models built around the concept of deep connection and low attachment. One of my favorite businesses employing this tactic is The Joint Chiropractic. Through extensive patient documentation and a connected network, these businesses enable patients like me to walk in to any location and experience a high degree of service, regardless of the professional who provides the service. Instead of being committed to one chiropractor in a specific location, I'm free to receive treatments (deep connection) with any provider in any location at any time (low attachment). Every time I go for a chiropractic adjustment, the service is always efficient and I enjoy connecting with new people. Over time, I've developed my favorite providers and locations, and I make a point to visit these places more frequently. But in general, I love the fact that no matter where I'm traveling, I can walk into a location without an appointment and get relief.

I equate the services and locations from a chiropractor to the man funnel. In this arrangement, I'm not exclusive to one—yet—but I am vetting and enjoying each as I go about my everyday life. If and when attachment occurs, it comes by invitation and a clear, mutual choice.

*"The point for me is to create relationships based on
deeper and more real notions of trust.
So that love becomes defined not by sexual exclusivity,
but by actual respect, concern, commitment to
act with kind intentions,
accountability for our actions,
and a desire for mutual growth."*
—DEAN SPADE

# CHAPTER TWENTY

## CONTRACTS AND COMMITMENT

While it sounds trite, there's an advantage to CYA (cover your ass), especially in business. No matter how great the relationship, the best, most fruitful business arrangements are protected with contracts outlining expectations, accountability, and payment terms. Presumably, both parties enter contracts with intention, trust, and provisions that support the partnership and outline the work to be completed. As discussed in the chapter on giving without strings, contracts also establish a foundation based on integrity, reduce the possibility of misunderstandings and ill feelings, and minimize the potential for either party to feel manipulated.

Contracts in business are equivalent to condoms in relationships, and I've been on all sides: using them for every interaction, raw dogging and enjoying it, having the best in place and still getting fucked, and being sick when choosing to go without. When it comes to having an orgasm, I've had my best experience when there's safety and clarity. Sometimes, that safety comes in the form of protection and condoms—especially when it's a partner I don't know all that well. With partners I love and know intimately, condoms and contracts are sometimes non-existent and safety looks and feels different.

I've found a tool that's helpful in creating safe and fruitful agreements —in business or relationships—that may or may not be inked in the form of a contract. You may have heard of the wildly popular book, *The Four Agreements: A Practical Guide to Personal Freedom, A Toltec Wisdom Book* by Don Miguel Ruiz. The information shared in Ruiz's book is revolutionary and should be taught in elementary schools and beyond. I've found when you have business and intimate relationships with people who keep all Four Agreements, the implicit contract created by the Agreements is just as valuable, if not more valuable, than the explicit one. Ruiz offers The Four Agreements as follows:

1. Be impeccable with your word.
2. Don't take anything personally.
3. Don't make assumptions.
4. Always do your best.

Three of my most fruitful and rewarding collaborations don't have contracts in place. One is the partnership I have with Jesse and Ultimate Vida. The second is the arrangement I have with the editor of my books. The third is a social media, design, website, and SEO company I use for personal and client work. In all cases, I have an incredible amount of respect for the business owners through the way they've demonstrated their integrity. When I met Mendi, co-owner of the website and SEO company for the first time, I was directing partnership activities for a media organization and selling sponsored content. Mendi submitted an article for sponsorship that was so well-written it could've been published without sponsorship or payment for those services. However, Mendi was quick to ensure our organization was paid for services rendered. He asked for the best rate, and he didn't even think about trying to get published under-the-radar without payment. Every time we collaborated, he was up-front with his expectations and followed through with his promises. In other words, he was impeccable with his word.

When Jesse and I were working to launch the Ultimate Vida course, I was still managing my recovery from 2020's global bitch slap. I was also navigating some very deep personal and ancestral healing. Trauma was surfacing at every turn and I wasn't exactly performing at my best. We had some very difficult and challenging conversations during that time. What I appreciated most about the safety Jesse created was that I could tell him exactly how I was feeling without holding anything back. While I was careful to take ownership of my own patterns and hang-ups, I loved the fact that Jesse was able to distance himself from my drama. In other words, he didn't take anything personally and he didn't make assumptions about my motives, expressions, or problems. He remained committed to the value I brought to the project and helped me to cultivate it.

My editor Sean has been a good friend for the past several years. When I asked him for some feedback on an article I wrote for *Refinery29*, he surprised me by giving it a full edit with commentary and suggestions for improvement. I wasn't expecting that amount of detail or dedication when I asked him to review it, but I was elated to receive it. He edits just like me. As hard as it can be to flesh out all of the editing details sometimes, it is refreshing to have someone go to such depth in the name of quality. I immediately hired him to edit my first book and used him a second time for this book, as well as many articles and collateral pieces in between. No matter what other priorities Sean has going on in his life, he gives my work the highest priority he can and continues to communicate with me throughout the process. As you can imagine, when working with projects that are so close to the chest, we've had some disagreements and tough convos over the years. No matter what, Sean always does his best.

When my partners embody the Four Agreements, it's easier to forgo a contract. In fact, contracts almost feel intrusive and insulting when you operate from love. Like condoms, I'm not opposed to contracts; I just don't want them to get in the way of a fruitful connection. I mean, condoms are designed to prevent reproduction. As someone who considers herself a mystic midwife helping others birth their creations, the last thing I want to do is stop the implantation of seeds that multiply and create prosperity.

I also prefer that the protection mechanism, whether contract or condom, doesn't replace the work of the Four Agreements. Even if things go badly with a person who embodies the Agreements, it's impossible to get screwed in a bad way. Why? Because those people are impeccable with their word. They don't take anything personally, don't make assumptions, and always do their best. In essence, they've done the work Ruiz's book explores.

It's much harder to have a tough conversation than it is to go silent, hide behind a contract provision, or fight a contract in court rather than working things out amicably. The people who meet me toe-to-toe with integrity, grace, presence, and reciprocation create a safety that's unparalleled—even compared to the tightest contract. I've been on both sides of this, as well. I've experienced contract "failures" with people who didn't employ the Agreements. When I say that, I'm including myself as one of the parties who wasn't always emotionally firm enough to fully carry out Ruiz's principles. Specifically, in those instances, I made assumptions and took things personally, which made it impossible to be objective. No matter how sound the contract, it's incredibly difficult to negotiate and move forward— together or separately—when all parties are not grounded and working with the Four Agreements.

And yet, when the Agreements serve as the basis for commitments and the contracts that go with them, it's nearly impossible to get it wrong— even in the most challenging situations. Of all the contracts that can be broken, I consider the marriage contract the most sacred and most potentially damaging for the divorcing parties. However, I honestly had the most amicable marital split ever. When I was getting divorced in 1997, I took it upon myself to write the divorce decree, detailing even the most specific information, particularly when it came to co-parenting. From an outsider's perspective, I was incredibly pleasant, giving, and probably naïve. Critics saw me giving my estranged husband everything he wanted. Many pointed out that I was too nice— that I shouldn't be so trusting—that I would ultimately be destroyed in the divorce. I stood firm in my positivity and trust.

The thing was, I wasn't aware of the Agreements back then. I was simply doing everything I could to ensure I would be awarded custody of my son. I couldn't imagine a life for either of us if we were not together. He was my literal and figurative world. I recall a good friend going through a divorce at the same time as me saying, "I don't know how you're getting through this with a kid." (Our son Johnathan was two years old at the time.) I replied, "I don't know how you're getting through without a child. Frankly, he's the reason I'm here." He was the only "capital T" Truth I had in my life. He served as my anchor, my reason for being, and sometimes the only reason I continued to live when I desperately wanted to die. I would've given anything and everything necessary to ensure he was by my side.

As nice as I was to Johnathan's dad during the divorce, I was keeping a secret. What others didn't see was the underhanded, manipulative, hidden agenda that ruled my interactions. During the initial stages of our separation, fear ruled me; I gave, not from love—but from fear. I also gave with the expectation of getting something in return. It was the exact opposite of the new understanding I presented in the chapter giving without strings. But hear me out, this experience set up the learning I needed to have a completely new understanding of how to give and protect myself simultaneously; how to later utilize the Four Agreements. In this older view, I thought if I gave my ex-husband everything he wanted, he would not fight for custody of our two-year-old son, Johnathan. My biggest fear was that I would lose my son in addition to my marriage. Mostly though, I feared I would lose what was left of me. Strangely, this fearful scheme resulted in a fabulous growth process for our entire family—one that bore bountiful fruits of caring, respect, loyalty, and love.

With empowerment, and more importantly, control in mind; I continued my sneaky plan by cooperating, negotiating, planning, and rearranging to meet everyone's needs. What I found was that the more I gave—of myself, my time and my resources—the more my husband gave in return. The real benefit though, was Johnathan's happiness. It wasn't long before my secret plan with a hidden agenda became a way of life—without the fraudulent intent. The more I acted out of love—rather than fear—the more genuine and peaceful the environment seemed.

As for the contract and the decree that I wrote? It became an awesome piece of documentation. Even when utilized, the best contracts are signed and never referred to again. Instead, the contract creates the terms both parties abide to and serves as a framework for the engagement. I recall my lawyer offering sage advice about our divorce contract stating, "Hopefully you never look at this decree again and you and your ex-husband talk through your needs and make changes on-the-fly as needed. However, in the event that doesn't happen and there's a disagreement, the contract serves as the record that will be held up in court." My ex and I revisited the decree to settle a disagreement or two, but for the most part, it served exactly as the lawyer described—protection and clarification that covered our asses. We never went to court once. He paid child support directly to me, once even writing an entire year's worth of post-dated checks I could cash as they came due. Remember, this was 1997—long before PayPal and Venmo were invented. We also privately renegotiated the amount of support on several occasions, and he continued to pay it until Johnathan graduated from high school, six months after his 18th birthday.

As hard as it was, even unaware of the principles Ruiz outlined in his book, we used the Four Agreements to manage every single interaction post-divorce. It's strange that the skills we need to carry out this give-and-take arrangement became suddenly adequate when the inadequacy of these same skills led to our failed marriage. Apparently, our spiritual gifts were meant to raise a beautiful son and surround him with love, not become one with one another. And the contract to do that came from the heart, creating a safety net for us individually and as a family. As the quote from the beginning of the chapter states, we operated from "actual respect, concern, commitment to act with kind intentions, accountability for our actions, and a desire for mutual growth."

*"When you stay too long, what should've been a graduation becomes a divorce."*
—ROB BELL

# CHAPTER TWENTY-ONE

## GRADUATIONS AND DIVORCES

When I think of graduations, I'm excited, grateful, and ready to celebrate. The most obvious and common graduations are those associated with education. They clearly mark one stage of life ending and another beginning. High school graduates leave the safety of their school and their longtime friends. Some jump to college, and others join the workforce. In either case, they're suddenly surrounded by new people, they're in new locations, or they're living independently. There's a delineated new path forward and a well-trod past that becomes a memory.

I've navigated some notable graduations in my life, including my Cum Laude college graduation at age 31 as a single mother working full-time and completing a full-time course load. Outside of education, the following "graduations" are also very near and dear to me: I graduated each time I elevated my corporate status through numerous promotions; I graduated from spending seven years in bed to walking daily and dancing every week; I graduated from the control of big pharma when I stopped taking nearly 1,000 prescription pills each month and became completely med-free; I graduated from the control of corporate employers when I became a grown-ass entrepreneur; I graduated from the control of substances when I released my addiction to them. Graduating from a victim mindset to one of complete personal ownership for my life backed and sustained every personal graduation.

My favorite personal graduation was taking the ultimate action to create the life of my dreams and move across the country. I sold the home I'd lived in for nearly 20 years, walked away from the only environment I'd ever known, and gave away all belongings except those that fit in my SUV. I left friendships, clients, family, and even my son in the name of self-care and personal dominion over my destiny. A few days before I left, I had brunch with my 22-year-old son Johnathan, who was recovering from a horrendous dance injury and broken ankle. He was in an awful place, unable to walk, unable to work, and living in a precarious spot. Other mothers in my family were surprised that I would choose my dreams over my son's immediate needs. At brunch, I told my son how much I loved him and wanted to see him succeed. I told him I trusted him to take care of himself and explained why I was leaving, even in his time of need. For me, leaving was a graduation from the pattern of martyrdom I'd learned from the family matriarchs. It was also a divorce from the idea that other people's needs must come before my own. I told him that I wanted him to see a different perspective of what it means to be a parent and how it's possible to operate from joy, freedom, and excitement over duty. His response still makes me giggle with pride. He said, "I respect the fuck out of you for that."

I'm happy to report he followed in my footsteps, moving to California a year after me. He often remarks that he wouldn't have had the courage to follow his dreams if I hadn't shown him the way. In California, my son created a life that's beyond the next-level. In his first year in RV sales, he started out-earning the salary it took me 25 years to build in the corporate world—and it keeps growing from there.

*When executed effectively,*
*our graduations can help others graduate too!*

The first time I heard the quote from Rob Bell, it struck me. "When you stay too long, what should've been a graduation becomes a divorce." I've been through a literal divorce between husband and wife. While it was very amicable and the best possible outcome for our entire family, it wasn't exactly fun.

I've had this problem of "trying" to leave relationships, personal and otherwise, staying, and then feeling stuck and losing a piece of me in the process. I did it with my husband; I did it in serious relationships after that; and I've done it with employers, clients, and friends. I wrote the following in an article for *Elephant Journal* in 2016 about personal graduations. This was before I'd moved to California and was written after I'd taken an epic solo road trip to scope out California living. The subject of my affection in this passage was the ex-boyfriend I did all the caretaking for—before I learned about feminine communication and giving without strings.

> *The relationship I'm grieving is the same one I tried to leave this time last year, and several times after that. Our love was hot and cold, but always passionate, intense, and chemically-rewarding.*

> *Earlier this year, I took a month-long Epic Solo Road Trip from the Midwest to California. The weekend before I left, we had a fabulous time together, dining, drinking, dancing, and having great sex. We were free, basking in love.*

> *By Saturday night, things were different. We didn't even discuss what was happening. When I left Sunday morning, he simply told me to come back to make sweet love, and he'd give me the best send-off.*

> *When I left for California as a single woman, I wrote a note to my (then) editor saying I needed to write an article about all relationships ending with cards, gifts, and blow jobs. What a graduation we had. It was a heartfelt and beautiful blessing to end our relationship.*

If only we would've truly ended our relationship, there, on the high note.

That's what graduations are to me—transitioning from one stage to another on a high note. Because I stayed too long in that relationship and countless others, I ended up with a ton of "divorces." In this case, I don't necessarily mean a literal divorce as in a husband and wife who go through the legal process of terminating their marriage. Here, I mean divorce as an agreement, engagement, or contract that *could've* ended well and didn't because the parties failed to speak up and split when the timing was right. In the case of my marriage, both were true. In all honesty, we should've parted ways before we got married, except I was too codependent to follow my intuitive nudges to separate. I'm grateful things worked out the way they did because I birthed a son through my marriage, and he is the best gift I've ever received. Our divorce went about as smoothly as it could have. As I mentioned earlier, I wrote the divorce decree, and we split the $500 cost for the attorney and court fees. Aside from the required court appearance to finalize the decree, we never once went to court to settle anything. To this day, my ex-husband and I continue to communicate and negotiate as co-parents to our now-adult son. Although we stayed too long in the relationship that ended in divorce, the way we managed it so amicably made it a graduation of sorts.

While the break-up of my marriage was tragic at the time, it caused me to renegotiate the way I planned to live my life and create a healthier environment for my son and me. I ended up buying a house on my own, and my son and I lived there for almost 20 years. I dedicated myself to raising my son as a single mom and growing my career in the insurance industry.

In my corporate job in insurance, I eventually knew I needed to graduate and do something new. I wasn't happy with the office environment and wasn't excited by the insurance world. Instead of parting ways from my job, when I realized the long and hard investment I made, I stayed. Looking for a new job was a lot of work and I was comfortable—a little too comfy, in fact. I made a good living, had amazing benefits, and made my own schedule as a department-of-one reporting to the CEO. Instead of graduating and moving to my next endeavor, I stayed too long, and the "graduation" became a "divorce" when my position was unexpectedly eliminated. After I received the news that I was let go, I was required to keep working for a few weeks to transition my workload. All the arrangements for my inevitable departure were managed very professionally by my employer and me. During this time, I continued to show up with integrity and did everything I could to set my successors (all 11 of them) up for success. I remember my boss—the same one who once asked me to tone down my sensitivity—being surprised at how well I maintained my emotional composure in my final days at work. My coworkers were surprised too, especially by the way I set them up for success sharing every bit of knowledge I had.

My job loss was a "divorce" that appeared as a blessing—not even in disguise. Much like the end of my marriage, the divorce with my employer was a catalyst in creating the space for me to follow my true passion and ultimately uproot everything I'd known to start my business and establish a new life in my dream location of Southern California. Even when divorces are unexpected and challenge the greatest levels of our existence, they can become celebrations and ceremonial graduations when approached with care, attention, and personal responsibility.

As an entrepreneur, I also experienced a client divorce in early 2020. It was an arrangement I should've graduated from, but because I didn't clearly speak up and create the proper transition plan, things ended abruptly, badly, and unnecessarily. In all honesty, after having such an abundant mindset, I became attached to the five-figure monthly income I was earning and was reluctant to give it up. While I initiated conversations about concerns and transition plans, they fell flat.

My heart hurts when I think about this divorce—even a full year after it happened. When I think about losing this client engagement, the recurring thought is, "I considered them family, and they essentially ghosted me." This particular client divorce triggered a primary abandonment wound in me. It also knocked me on my ass—financially, professionally, and emotionally. As terrible as that sounds, it was a beautiful thing in the end because it caused me to search for ways to heal the wound that played in the background of my mind, despite my various successes, all of my life.

Graduations and divorces are part of life. At a glance, one seems positive and the other negative. However, I believe every situation can create positive change in our lives, especially when we are open to learn the lessons that arrive through them, heed the opportunities presented, and remain open to new players and new collaborations.

*"Life is rhythm that must be understood.*
*I feel the rhythm,*
*I let it lead and I consent."*
—NIKOLA TESLA

# CHAPTER TWENTY-TWO

## THE UNIVERSE LEADS

Most people dream of "having it all." It's a potent desire we all share. The exact meaning of "having it all" varies from person to person. Yet, it's safe to say that having the freedom to live and work on your own terms is at the top of every entrepreneur's list. Add epic love and immense wealth to that freedom, and I'd say that's a good recipe for "having it all."

Decades ago, one of my mentors told me, "I never said you couldn't have it all. I just didn't say you could have it all at once." Herein lies the problem. Particularly for entrepreneurs, there's a tendency to put all of our focus on growing a business. Personally, I wonder if it's possible to have both epic love *and* a growing business. And yet, we've heard from entrepreneurs like Cliff and Marta who not only have both, but they have both with each other. They're building empires and immense wealth side-by-side, and they have the freedom to live where they want, and to work by their own rules.

Others, like me, aren't exactly there yet. We may experience one or two components of the trifecta that includes love, wealth, and freedom. But we may have a challenging time balancing and maintaining all three at once. So, in the absence of "having it all," and on the way to achieving our greatest passions, how do we maintain the stamina to keep pursuing love, wealth, and freedom?

This is where things come full circle for me. In early 2020, just before the COVID-19 pandemic shut down the world, I published my first book, *TranscenDANCE: Lessons from Living, Loving, and Dancing.* I often say this book was a gift, as the theme—allowing the Universe to lead your dance with life—was downloaded from my highest self. At the time I wrote it, I hadn't personally embodied all of the book's concepts. In all honesty, it was no surprise to me that the very day I uploaded my book, the five-figure monthly retainer I'd been earning the prior 18 months was canceled without warning. On the day I was expecting to be paid $11,000, I was suddenly and completely out of work because I'd been working exclusively for one client. Initially, I wasn't all that worried because I was preparing to launch *Transcen-DANCE* workshops and dance party events, which felt like very aligned work to me. Then, COVID put a stop to all events.

You know what they say about what you ask for? You can't always get what you want, but you always get what you need. When you ask the Universe to lead your dance, you're not given a perfect dance. Instead, you're given opportunities to accept the lead and follow a new rhythm.

The thing about letting the Universe lead your dance is that you must relinquish control. You must allow the lead to pull you in new directions you didn't expect. You must allow the lead to steer you clear of directions and moves that aren't working and don't fit the dance you were born for. When the Universe leads, your dance will include brand new steps that require practice and patience. Let me tell you, I love dancing. But, allowing the Universe to lead my dance with entrepreneurship, life, and love was exceptionally challenging. My mental state was so poor, I literally could not work throughout most of 2020. The majority of my time was spent battling the worst suicidal ideation I'd ever encountered. It was honestly a moment-to-moment exercise in staying alive and choosing to remain on this earth. Any attempts at love were just repeating patterns of self-sabotage and briefly and unproductively engaging in trauma bonds.

What I wanted was epic love and immense wealth. What I got was a global pandemic, unemployment wages at a tiny fraction of what I was accustomed to, a lockdown that rendered dancing with a crowd impossible, and…freedom.

Yes, you read that right. I gained freedom in 2020. You see, in order to have the life of my dreams, I had to become someone and something I'd never fully embraced. I had to become *me*. That's a lot more challenging than it sounds. Becoming me required abandoning the version of me who did everything to earn love and achieve wealth. As part of that, I had to cultivate my own love, temporarily relinquish wealth, and rely on God. It required exercising profound vulnerability, facing the deepest, darkest shadows of myself, making peace with my inner child, confronting my ego, and learning to self-soothe for the first time in my life.

This immense amount of unraveling I did in 2020 enabled me to be so free that I felt safe to be me no matter what. That meant showing up in business as my quirky, foul-mouthed tattooed self, armed with effective solutions, outlandish ideas, and meticulous execution. It also meant showing up consistently with high value and accepting nothing less than high-value partners, whether in the bedroom or the boardroom. It meant getting vulnerable and sharing my heart, even when I was afraid I'd be abandoned for doing so. It also meant accepting that when abandonment occurs, taking care of myself and understanding that the loss simply equals a lack of alignment—nothing more and nothing less.

I now understand the freedom I gained by addressing my shadow to be a pre-requisite to *TranscenDANCE*. It's also a precursor to living your Ultimate Vida, but we'll get to that in a bit. Here's an overview of *TranscenDANCE* from the book itself:

*TranscenDANCE is the process of surrendering to the lead of the Universe. It's a deep knowing, a resonance of unwavering faith, and a compelling pull forward to your highest calling. It's being poised to dance with life as it comes. It's remaining present, staying in the moment, and navigating life one step at a time. It's knowing each move and opening is created for the highest good of all parties. It's allowing the Universe to move through you and expressing your true self.*

*TranscenDANCE requires trust and faith beyond any you've ever experienced. It's a slow, deep unravelling of everything you've known to reveal the greatest inner brilliance you can imagine. This light is your soul within, once dimmed by expectations, conditioning, contrasting situations, limiting beliefs, bullshit rules, and incessant fears. The more you surrender to the unknown while maintaining your soul's center, moving with grace, and staying in joy, the easier it is to accept and follow the lead of the Universe.*

*TranscenDANCE requires periods of movement and rest to shed layer upon layer of indoctrination, self-sabotage, and patterns that do not serve your development. This healing will challenge and test you to make sure you're resilient and able to sustain your life's huge calling. At the point you think you'll break down, you'll surrender more, and you'll break through.*

*TranscenDANCE is a process of honoring the dark, embracing your shadow, and accepting your imperfections in order to shine more brightly. For a long time, I chose not to acknowledge my darkness and imperfections—not realizing they were completely visible to everyone but me. This led to a very disjointed life and a failure to accept myself, my past, and my purpose. I learned that it's not possible to remain healthy while denying myself. Failing to care for myself while ignoring my passion kept me in an endless cycle of dis-ease. In order to fly, I had to surrender to the process. Essentially, TransenDANCE is metamorphosis akin to a caterpillar becoming a butterfly.*

*People who've completed TranscenDANCE are open to receive, allowing the gifts of life's flow, appreciating every offering, and then asking for more. They know with certainty they're worthy of receiving everything they desire and more. They move with freedom and fluidity surrendering to and relying on the lead of the Universe.*

Wow. I have tears and chills reading that today. The process of TranscenDANCE completely describes the experience I had in 2020. Every single detail is accounted for. I've always believed that we can write our future. I just didn't realize it was my future self writing it—until now. What freedom!

TranscenDANCE is the basis for the personal freedom we need to show up as orgasmic entrepreneurs too. Jesse Panama, the creator of Ultimate Vida, received some amazing advice from his therapist a few years ago that is relevant for the love component of the trifecta of having it all. This is how he described it to me:

*I remember a while back, being in a dark space and speaking with my therapist about the theme of love. At that point, I had a failed marriage, several relationships and flings that didn't last, and a period of serial dating. I was feeling that I'd never find my soulmate. She asked me what lights me up. What do I see as my calling or purpose? I told her about Ultimate Vida, of course. And she basically said "So just go build Ultimate Vida! Living and being on purpose is by far the best way to attract the woman of your dreams."*

I'm elated to report this strategy works and Jesse is proof. On January 25, 2021, I was a guest at Jesse's wedding when he married, Krysthel —the woman of his dreams. Of course, the wedding was conducted via Zoom because of the pandemic. Computer screens didn't make the ceremony any less meaningful or idyllic, though. The multicultural aspect of the wedding was simply beautiful as people from all over the world attended to celebrate their love. The virtual wedding guests were family and community members Jesse gathered while living and traveling all over the world and building his business, Ultimate Vida.

That leaves the last component of "having it all"—wealth. And let's not forget that wealth without freedom can be a prison. Even when work comes with golden handcuffs, they are still handcuffs. Honestly, I much prefer handcuffs in the bedroom than at work.

If you're not sure how to break free from the prison of an overwhelming work schedule, a lackluster love life, and the freedom to live and work on your own terms, I invite you to consider Ultimate Vida as the greatest dance party there is.

*"A tribe is a group of people connected to one another, connected to a leader, and connected to an idea. For millions of years, human beings have been part of one tribe or another. A group needs only two things to be a tribe: a shared interest and a way to communicate."*
—SETH GODIN

# CHAPTER TWENTY-THREE

## SELF-ACTUALIZATION AND SECURITY
### BY FEATURED AUTHOR JESSE PANAMA

Iconic author and entrepreneur Seth Godin stated on the Tim Ferriss podcast that the completion rate for online courses is a startling 3%. Does this mean that the life's work of brilliant writers and teachers goes in vain 97% of the time, and that we as consumers of information are incapable of taking action on what we learn? Well, left to our own devices, the answer is sadly, "Yes," the vast majority of the time. How many books and courses have you purchased but failed to act on what you learned, or even finished reading? For me, the answer is far higher than I'd care to admit!

But thankfully, there's a simple and stunningly powerful solution to dramatically increase your odds of success from a paltry 3% all the way up to just about 50/50! According to a study by the online learning platform NovoEd, course students who are also part of an online community have a 16 times higher completion rate than those who go it alone![1] In fact, were it not for the power of community, you would not be reading these words right now. Melissa and I connected in a Facebook group, and as it happens, that same group led to me being flown to Barcelona to teach the Ultimate Vida to freedom seekers from all corners of the globe.

It's not just about completion rates, quantitative success, or expanding your network, though. It's about something even deeper and more important: happiness. Consider the following story shared by author James Clear in his article "How to Be Happy: A surprising lesson on happiness from an African tribe:"[2]

> *There was an anthropologist who had been studying the habits and culture of a remote African tribe.*
>
> *He had been working in the village for quite some time and the day before he was to return home, he put together a gift basket filled with delicious fruits from around the region and wrapped it in a ribbon. He placed the basket under a tree and then he gathered up the children in the village.*
>
> *The man drew a line in the dirt, looked at the children, and said, "When I tell you to start, run to the tree and whoever gets there first will win the basket of the fruit."*
>
> *When he told them to run, they all took each other's hands and ran together to the tree. Then they sat together around the basket and enjoyed their treat as a group.*
>
> *The anthropologist was shocked. He asked why they would all go together when one of them could have won all the fruits for themselves?*
>
> *A young girl looked up at him and said, "How can one of us be happy if all the other ones are sad?"*

Let's start with the hard, cold facts that we can easily calculate. My last tribal experience? It's conservatively led to over half a million dollars in verifiable business, and that's not even counting additional business from connections made through the community. And that was from paying $97 per month for two years for a community membership. So, a $2,328 investment for at least $500,000 in business? That's an astronomical 21,400% return on my investment or, $214 back for every dollar invested.

It's not like I aggressively pitched to close this business, either. It came from simply showing up, connecting, adding value, and winning the trust of fellow group members. Oh, and this $500,000 is hardly a thing of the past. Several of the revenue streams are ongoing to this day, and this doesn't even count an equity position I have in a business I connected with through my membership. When all is said and done, I fully expect that $500,000 to expand into several million dollars from the same $2,328 investment.

But you know what's even more remarkable?

As significant as the financial rewards were, they can't begin to hold a candle to the priceless ways in which this very same membership enriched my life. That company I mentioned, in which I have an equity position? The majority owner has become one of my dearest friends in the world, as has his wife. We have spent time together in Wales, Greece, China, and the US. And a few years ago, when I was in a really dark place? They invited me to fly over and celebrate the holidays with them, which lifted my spirits during a very painful time. I will never forget it.

Several of my other marketing and coaching clients came through this same group as well. And quite a few more from this community became very dear friends and were highlighted in the acknowledgments of my book, where I paid tribute to those most important to me. I have laughed and cried and shared countless unforgettable moments with these friends whom the organization connected me with. This is what I live for, and it's quite literally priceless to me.

As life-changing as this association was for all the reasons I just mentioned? It was lacking one crucial element: The ability for its members to create financial security through partnership.

Sure, the organization had referral contests from time to time where they gave away prizes for those who referred the newest members. But this was a major missed opportunity in my view.

Some people referred dozens or even hundreds of new members! Imagine if those membership fees were generously shared with the referrers on an ongoing basis! Instead of winning things like iPads or weekend getaways (which are cool and all, don't get me wrong), they could have earned a steady monthly income which could be a car payment, a rent or mortgage payment, or even full-time income, depending on how many members they referred. In other words, life-changing money.

*We've Got You Covered, and We'd Be Honored if You'd Join Us.*

At my company, Ultimate Vida, we are not going to make that mistake. We are going to share the wealth with you—forever.

Sure, we'll give you all the tools you need to build your own ecosystem, get free, and live the life of your dreams. The book, *The Art of Freedom,* lays out the blueprint. The course fills in the details, and the community will give you an astounding 16 times higher chance of succeeding, as we've already uncovered.

But what if once you're inside the UV community, you find yourself loving our training and emphasis on self-actualization and living an optimized life, but discover that instead of building your own platform, ecosystem, and online business, you'd rather bring people into the UV community to share the experience with you—and get paid while we take care of all the details?

For this opportunity, both you and I have Melissa to thank. When I was on a call with her to coach her on her marketing and strategy, I asked her "How do you envision monetizing your book? What would you like your readers to do next?" She stunned me by answering "If it's ok with you, I'd like to invite them into the Ultimate Vida community, because I believe it will give them everything they need."

We'd be deeply honored to have you in the community, we promise to give you everything we've got to help you live a freedom-based, self-actualized life, and we'd love to cut you some sizeable checks as well!

See you on the inside,

Jesse

*"When you have clarity and commit to manifesting your heart's desire, you will be drawn to those who light you up on every level... and they will be drawn to you."*
—ANNETTE VAILLANCOURT

# CHAPTER TWENTY-FOUR

## MANIFESTING LOVE

I wholeheartedly believe in the message of my TEDx Talk, "The Dance of Collaboration." However, as evidenced in the crash I took after I delivered it, something was off for me. I even wondered whether or not the thing that felt most aligned in my life was actually aligned with my life's path. There's no question that collaboration, my TEDx Talk's theme, is the way to our abundant future. However, much like my first book, the talk was delivered from my future self and I hadn't exactly caught up fully with its message yet. I had some work to do before I could fully appreciate the views I expressed—especially because I now understand the concepts presented were ahead of their time—or at least, ahead of *my own timing*.

The thing about changing the world, is you can't really do it until you've effectively transformed your own experience. When I delivered the talk, I hadn't done any of the intense work to resolve personal ancestral traumas like the work I did in 2020. I'd come a very long way from my severely depressed days where I literally spent seven years in bed and took nearly 1,000 prescription pills every month. Yes, I'd been med-free for years, moved across the country to follow my dreams, and even made several of my own dreams come true. Yet, there were still lingering doubts in my mind that clouded my ability to go after the thing my heart wanted more than anything: love. More specifically, I was holding out for a reciprocal partnership and business. If I was ever going to invest 100% of my heart in something again, it certainly wasn't going to be insurance or a corporate job. I wanted to invest in me, in love, and in a future that creates a literal and lasting impact for myself and others.

Once I took a deep dive into healing my wounds, my world and heart opened to a completely different perspective of my TEDx Talk. Suddenly, I was open to new ways to collaborate on my own accord and with others. I could also see the increased benefits for the collective through personal healing. In addition to providing a personal breakthrough and helping me address my shadow, ego, and inner child wounds, my NLP training class gave me a far greater return than my own personal transformation. A special person I met in the class introduced me to a brand-new community of friends and soul family who not only assisted in my continued healing, but brought an entirely new perspective of collaboration into my life. You know what's better? This family came complete with a new and built-in community of souls aligned with my life's path. Members of my soul family magnetized to me as I healed.

An unexpected conversation around the benefits of plant medicine connected me intimately to Mayra, another student of NLP. She's a beautiful and engaging single mother who instantly became a best friend. In our class, the instructor often remarked that Mayra was the perfect example of how to express gratitude. No matter the circumstances, Mayra remained appreciative, focused on her vision, and was grateful for every ounce of support that appeared in her life. It wasn't just the support she welcomed either. She was grateful for the contrast, too. Her loving, inquisitive, and unassuming energy drew me in. Very quickly, Mayra took me under her wing and invited me to ceremonies and events where I met some amazing healers. Around ritual circles, I received profound healing that touched my soul's greatest depths, releasing lifetimes of generational trauma, and assisting me with increased alignment for further manifestation. While this isn't the place or time to detail my journey with plant medicine, for now, I'll say it's the most intense and profound work I've ever done. I'm also committed to helping others through this healing modality. While pivotal in the result, plant medicine is just a small part of manifesting love though.

When Mayra told me about Maricruz, an indigenous woman groomed from a young age to be a healer, a new opening appeared. Maricruz has a vision to heal individuals by coordinating their mind, body, and spirit for optimal health. Much like the message I shared in my TEDx Talk, her desire is to change lives, inspire others, and ultimately, unite the world. When I met Maricruz for the first time, I wept as she shared her vision to gather and connect healers. Even via Zoom, I had such deep resonance with her message, energy, and vision that my body couldn't contain the vibration. Tears poured from my eyes and my heart broke open. In that moment, the message of my TEDx Talk came full circle. Collaboration most certainly is the way to our abundant future. And, healing ourselves and others is an incredibly effective, fun, and loving way to get there. The ceremonial circles of healing also create an instant community for collaboration, integration, and expansion.

A few months after my introduction to Maricruz, she hosted a gathering of healers at an oasis in Desert Hot Springs. I honestly wasn't feeling the best that day and considered not even attending. Mayra stood by with support saying, "I don't know what to expect, but I think it's important for us to show up and be present to whatever is available for us."

Within moments of my arrival, I saw him. I was instantly curious. When we struck up a conversation, the first thing he asked was, "What are you dedicated to?" I was so surprised and smitten by the depth of his inquiry, I stumbled a bit with my response and blurted out something like, "Healing. First for myself, and then for others."

As synchronicity would have it, he was a healer.

Oh, damn! How fortunate was I? I refrained from asking him to remove my nagging headache and excruciating neck pain and went about enjoying the event.

After a transformative hands-on healing session from Maricruz, the healer named Idelfonso gave me a hug and began chatting with me. We walked on the sacred grounds and reveled in the power of the desert vortex, while sharing our secrets and connecting from a place of wholeness. It was apparent to me from our very first conversation that he's done his work. When talking about his life experiences and other people, he never shared from a place of blame. Even with challenging circumstances and events, his recollection was one of ownership, confirming, "Yes, they did that, but I allowed it." We laid under the stars talking about everything imaginable until the wee hours of the morning.

We haven't stopped talking since.

I found the one I love, the one who makes me safe, and the one I feel most at home with. He is a reflection of me and the one who holds the mirror to remind me of my beauty, spark my intelligence, and challenge me to own my power. The admiration and appreciation are mutual, reciprocal, and abundant. Intuitively connected and cosmically guided, we have the same goals and dreams, and we are now passionately pursuing them together. I've always desired a romantic match that's a true partnership. I dreamed of being the power couple who has one another's back, grows together, and leads others through coaching and spiritual leadership. Suddenly, and without warning, my reality began matching my dreams.

Within two weeks of our first meeting, we were booked to facilitate a workshop at a large healing festival together. From there, the opportunities expanded and have continued to grow. That's the way alignment works. I'm so excited about the future, and I cannot wait to see how things unfold. Meanwhile, I'm standing in gratitude and am full of pride for overcoming everything that brought me to this point.

I remember when Beth first met Tosca in 2017. Immediately after their first date, Beth sent me a message about their date, telling me she met a grown-ass woman and said her face hurt from laughing and smiling so much. As their relationship quickly and beautifully blossomed before my eyes, Beth frequently described their connection with phrases like, "She is amazing, I can't believe how legitimately lucky I am to have been found by her in this life."

The thing is, I don't believe in luck. I believe the abundance that's "automagically" created and often defined as luck, is acquired through the choices we deliberately make, the beliefs we hold dear, and the work we do.

Because Beth and I were friends when she went through her period of questioning and came out on the other side of her experience in her power and showing up as her quirky self, the power of alignment that magnetized Tosca to her was easy for me to see. I promptly told Beth, "You're not lucky. You made a decision that served you well. You worked for this—and yet it was effortless at the same time. You just finally met a grown-ass woman worthy of what you have to offer. You absolutely deserve it." Her response still cracks me up. She said, "Holy fuck, ain't that the truth?"

Here's the biggest truth bomb in the message I gave Beth. "You absolutely deserve it." After her extensive self-exploration and healing, Beth believed it too!! For anyone looking to manifest love, I'd say that's the number one value. In 2020, I had the perfect opportunity to address the deliberate choices I was making and the beliefs I held dear. Many of the beliefs I was carrying were the opposite of being deserving, worthy, and enough. Each limiting belief was faced, addressed, and shed or meticulously removed or rewired. Next, I cultivated what remained. In short, I did the work. It was work that excavated everything that made me feel less deserving of what I desired. At nearly 50 years old, I can honestly say it was the first time I learned to truly feel my feelings and soothe my emotions without numbing them. I made it through the pandemic, arguably one of the most challenging times in history, completely alone, without an income, and absent vices like alcohol, sex, and drugs. It was one of the biggest "wins" of my entire life. In fact, I won my life by deliberately choosing to live in every moment. I can see now this process of becoming was also an "offering" toward the life I wanted to manifest.

A few weeks before I met Idelfonso, there was a meme floating around that said, "Someone out there is manifesting you." I reveled in the idea of that and got excited about arriving as a manifestation in someone else's life rather than waiting to manifest someone in my life. The night we met, Idelfonso said, "I'm mesmerized by you. I manifested you." Earlier that day, he told Maricruz he knew he was going to meet someone special at the event. I knew I was going to meet someone special, too, I just didn't know when or where. While waiting for the special connection to appear, I worked on me and remained open to love arriving. Not surprisingly, that's the primary message of *Transcen-DANCE*. When Idelfonso and I talked about the book you're reading now and the messages it contains, it was clear to both of us that he's a manifestation of what I wrote. Writing and healing the wounds of my past created a new clarity for my future and invited it to arrive. Once it arrived, I allowed it to literally move me.

Recently, when sharing the news of my new love with a family member who has been married more than 40 years, I told her that Idelfonso and I are "crazy intuitive together." She said, "Sounds like a good fit. Aren't you glad you did so much work before you met him?" I replied, "There's no way I would've met him without doing the work. You know what's better? He's done the work too! We are very much equals."

> *In order to meet the person I wanted to love,*
> *I had to **become** the person I wanted to love.*

That includes loving and accepting every part of who I am, removing shame, abolishing guilt, addressing limiting beliefs, integrating conflicting parts, telling the truth, showing up in authenticity, and expectantly allowing things to unfold.

I can't stress enough how important doing the inner work and learning accountability were to *allowing* true, resonant, and reciprocal love to arrive in my life. Sadly, I more frequently pushed away love and support than I invited it in, thanks to a primary abandonment wound. When love and support did appear, it was rare for me to truly receive it. In my NLP class, one of my subconscious programs, "love is not to be trusted," reared its ugly head. Working with JoJo, the featured author who introduced the unveiling wholeness chapter of this book, revealed a primary limiting belief of "I'm not safe." This was the fundamental reason why, for so much of my life, I'd self-sabotage nearly every "favorable" opportunity for love and success that came my way. It's also the same reason I sometimes get scared of how comfortable and at home I feel with Idelfonso.

Quite honestly, with a history of trauma, having a safe place to land with an overflow of love and support can be more uncomfortable than comfortable—hence, my long-standing pattern of not being able to maintain it. This is precisely why completing the work to create safety within was essential for love to arrive and to generate the ability to maintain it. As discussed in Chapters 7 and 8, relationships are fertile ground to address triggers and grow from them. And believe me, Idelfonso and I trigger one another on the daily. We also safely process the triggers with care, coming out the other side of each conversation with a new understanding and often, new agreements, too. Even before I met Idelfonso, I could tell I was really healing when the people I was surrounded by were actively doing the work of healing. My collaborations were expanding to reflect the healing I'd completed. I could have challenging conversations with other adults without fear of retribution or abandonment.

Beyond personal relationships, the right community of people are essential to further our personal satisfaction and success. But, the responsibility for healthy responses extends beyond our own internal happiness. Dr. Nicole LePera said it best in her book *How To Do The Work*, when she said, "Our internal state of mind is often mirrored by those around us, making our inner worlds contagious; when we feel safe, others feel safe."

It's both exciting and terrifying to think about my inner world as contagious. Because of the challenges I experienced in 2020, I'm incredibly grateful the year was spent in solitary quarantine. There's no way I wanted anyone else to experience the dark, pure hell I endured as I confronted my shadow, inner child, and ego in the name of healing. That's why I essentially pulled back from everything, including a complete and total social media detox for over two weeks (which was a Herculean effort for me, since I live and work on social media every single day).

On the other side of the darkness, I'm experiencing a light, a joy, and an intrigue that I've never known. I'm deeply in love—with myself, with God, with Idelfonso, with my soul family, with my purpose, and with the communities I'm building. I would love nothing more than for this love, this joy, this light, and this intrigue to be as contagious as the virus that stimulated the pandemic and my healing. Imagine how different our world would be if more people operated from a place of authenticity, deep connection, and personal growth. Imagine how different our lives would be if more businesses operated from a place of authenticity, deep connection, and personal growth.

I often tell Mayra that she's the best $6,000 I ever spent. That's the cost of the NLP course I took. Given the exponential way my world, my heart, and my business expanded from that one connection alone, I'm beyond grateful I took the leap to invest in me.

When we invest in ourselves, and continue to persist, despite the fear, despite the challenges, and despite the pain, we are rewarded beyond measure.

*"Love is not just an enabler for success;*
*love **is** success.*
*The real work of your life is to know how to love and*
*be loved. There is no greater work than this."*
—ROBERT HOLDEN, PH.D.

# CHAPTER TWENTY-FIVE

# LIVING YOUR MANIFESTATION

Manifesting the life, business, bank account, and love of my dreams isn't nearly as challenging as maintaining it can be. I can't count how many times I quickly and effortlessly manifested exactly what I was looking for, only to watch it slip through my hands in short order.

Reading that quote from Robert Holden, PhD, "The real work of your life is to know how to love and be loved. There is no greater work than this," sends shivers down my spine today.

Being in a committed relationship after years of being single proved to be far more challenging than I expected. I imagined after being "bone dry" and devoid of intimacy for so long, I would soak up all the love that poured in and allow it to overflow. Unfortunately, that's not how it worked out—at least not in the long term. It was beyond disappointing.

There are two main reasons why I've been reluctant to write this additional and final chapter. 1) As much as I shunned Hallmark and other romantic movies because they don't always feel realistic to me when everything works out and is tied up with a neat bow by the end, I've really come to appreciate happy endings. Although I understand the realities of life, I also believe in magic and I still dream about my happily ever after. 2) I know intimately the power of the written word. I watched the challenging message of my first book unfold before my eyes within moments of publishing it. I also experienced the manifestation of the call for love I wrote about in this book before I'd finished writing it.

Because of this, I wanted to be incredibly intentional with the words I put into the Universe—especially when it comes to my livelihood and my love life. The biggest message I've received as I've been on this journey of entrepreneurship and personal healing is related to the way I view my *true* value and worth. Owning my value and worth is also the key component to manifesting. When I show up as me, in my power, and utilizing my gifts, knowing I'm deserving, I can manifest nearly anything I desire. I've demonstrated this time and time again and it's so much fun.

However, as soon as I compromise or lose that connection to my own power, living my manifestation gets challenging. I've proved this time and time again as well. The challenges show up at both ends of the spectrum too. Either it's hard to maintain things that are truly aligned like love, health, and wealth, or it's hard to release and walk away from manifestations that don't feel good or are no longer aligned like dates, client work, coping mechanisms, and survival patterns.

*As soon as I place value outside of myself,*
*I lose the ability to remain true to who I am.*
*The truth of who I am is infinite, loving, and abundant.*

This truth is one of the main concepts Kyle Cease wrote about in his book, *The Illusion of Money*. Especially when it comes to entrepreneurship, social media, and digital marketing, it's easy to associate worth with the amount of money earned, the prestigious clients served, and/or the high value daters attracted. Except there's a huge disadvantage to linking worth to money and other people. When we lose money, clients, and relationships, we can feel lost too. Cease confronts this by acknowledging our true value, stating: "Your value is not what you have in the bank or your job or your business connections. Your true value is based on how closely connected to yourself you are. It's about how much access you have to the infinite nature of your being."

I promise you, in early 2020, when I lost my dream client that I considered family, I was lost. Probably more lost than I've ever been in my life and certainly way more lost than I was when I was released from my corporate career of 25 years. Why? Because I put my heart into my position and I externalized my power. Working exclusively with one client who I saw as more powerful than me, I became dependent on them, financially and otherwise. I constantly worried about losing them. I failed to speak up for my needs because I feared I'd lose the contract and they'd abandon me. There's destruction in dependency, mostly because it can cause a disconnection from Source energy. Rather than cultivating the power I had within, I outsourced it to my client; which is funny considering they outsourced work to me.

Robert Holden, PhD., addresses the basis for the ability to access our infinite nature in his book *Loveability: Knowing How to Love and Be Loved*, offering the following,

> *When you know that your source of love is not outside you, you don't stalk people, put them on pedestals, or turn them into idols. You treat people as equals. You don't put on a show. You express yourself without trying to win approval. You don't give love to get love. You love unconditionally, without attaching emotional invoices. You make good choices about whom to give your phone number to, whom to date, when to have sex or not, whom to be friends with, and when it's authentic to stay in a relationship or leave. When we understand our worth and value isn't tied to one client or even a specific business, or business activity, it's easier to be true to ourselves. Being true to who we are and true to the mission we're here to accomplish helps provide us greater ease in accomplishing our goals, earning money, and attracting partners.*

I've experienced this first hand. When I moved to California, I hadn't lined up enough client work to pay the bills. But, I was ridiculously connected to who I was and the purpose I'd fulfill. A day after I arrived, a consulting arrangement that was in the works fell through. I wasn't worried. Honestly. I knew I'd find clients and be able to serve them well. On the drive out to SoCal, I had a number of ideas on how to better serve one of my existing clients. I knew that implementing my ideas for the client could be mutually beneficial. I also understood it to be a short-term arrangement and one that would help me get further on the path to my purpose. I did amazing work for them, but my worth wasn't tied to the position or the work I did. This allowed me to show up in my full authority and take feedback "effortlessly." Even criticism didn't penetrate me because I understood that while they were the client who paid my bills, I wasn't dependent on them. I knew I had value beyond what I offered the organization. Because of this, I was never afraid to speak up, speak my mind, or be emotional when I was moved to do so.

When it came to my budding relationship with Idelfonso, a new factor bubbled to the surface and complicated things. The thing about trauma is that the body stores it. It's not just personal trauma either, our bodies become giant receptacles, hosting the trauma of multiple generations of ancestors.

As much work as I'd done and the extensive lengths I went to in removing trauma from my experience, it was quickly evident that the triggers encountered in my new relationship activated my stored trauma in a way I did not expect or experience before. I credit even the ability to feel the activation and new body pain to the fact that I'd stopped numbing myself. During the pandemic, I learned to self-soothe for the first time in my life—at the ripe age of 49. I went through the horrors of a global pandemic, unemployment, and suicidal ideation completely alone. I also did it free of prior coping mechanisms of medication, alcohol, recreational drugs, binge-eating, and casual sex.

According to Bessel A. Van der Kolk, author of *The Body Keeps the Score: Brain, Mind, and Body in the Healing of Trauma*, I'd done the hard work of coming into communion with my body. He addresses self-soothing and the exact methods I'd employed in 2020 stating, "Self-regulation depends on having a friendly relationship with your body. Without it you have to rely on external regulation—from medication, drugs like alcohol, constant reassurance, or compulsive compliance with the wishes of others." I started paying attention to my body, fed it healthy foods, gave it adequate sleep, and exercised consistently. I had a new baseline for health and the data to back it up: a 40-pound weight loss, decreased resting heart rate, increased heart rate variability, consistent sleep, normalized glucose levels, better nervous system responses with less time spent in fight or flight, and a vastly improved cardio fitness level.

Because of this, when the excruciating pain showed up in my shoulders and heart chakra, it was easy to notice. Very quickly, the thing I loved most about being in a relationship with Idelfonso became the thing that hurt me the most—and I mean that quite literally. Growth, I've come to find, is realized as we acknowledge our own triggers and make the choice to address them in a new way. Relationships provide a fast track to growth because they constantly trigger us. When my relationship began, I reveled in the triggers, racking up new choices and redeeming growth like I was playing a video game where each resolved trigger offered super powers and new life. It was beautiful and the love was ever present.

Then, new levels of the projected video game appeared and the triggers got deeper—deeper than the ocean deep, and several generations back. In a short period of time, Idelfonso and I did several healings together, including a healer's retreat accessing the powerful vortexes in Sedona, a plant medicine ceremony, and a sweat lodge session in a Mexican *Temezcal*. Through this work, it was obvious to me—and others who attended—that the healing we were undertaking had as much, if not more, to do with our stored trauma, generational lineage, and the dysfunctional family dynamics my partner and I respectively grew up with, than our real-time relationship experience. Nonetheless, we had a bigger picture in mind. Best-selling author and Relational Life Institute founder Terry Real explains the value of such dedication to ancestral healing and the gifts it offers noting, "Family dysfunction rolls down from generation to generation, like a fire in the woods, taking down everything in its path until one generation has the courage to turn and face the flames. That person brings peace to their ancestors and spares the children that follow." Through our healing work, we were facing the flames like warriors, and we practically got swallowed by them in the process. Plus, glimpses of horrific and dark repressed memories came through for me.

That's when the game changed. Any time I'd get triggered, my body became instantly inflamed and activated. It was excruciating. His triggers were lit up, too, and suddenly, instead of observing and supporting one another's triggers with distance, compassion, and love, we were in the thick of them. Worse, Idelfonso and I had conversations loaded with projections and blame—our childhood wounds exposed and hemorrhaging.

Here's where I did two things: a step towards evolution and the other backward in a familiar pattern. First, I recognized how unsafe I felt in my body and did something to rectify it. I could feel myself falling into the same relationship pattern that haunted me my whole life, which is one of self-abandonment and taking personal responsibility for the emotions and reactions of others. As much as my heart was attached, my body was literally screaming at me to detach. It was clear that I was outsourcing my power in love—and my body was constantly alerting me of the discontent. The difference between this time and all the other times before, I understood that the source of love, commitment, and contentment didn't reside outside of me. I had no choice but to end the relationship to protect my own source. Maybe for the first time ever in a relationship, I listened to my body's intuitive wisdom and took action based on what it was calling me to do.

While I'm proud of this step in the right direction and the evolution for my soul, it's clear in hindsight that I also repeated a different pattern—I ran. I stopped playing the game altogether. I didn't have a proper conversation. I simply said "I feel unsafe" and walked away. There was no discussion, no support, and no grace. I abandoned him, the love we enjoyed, and the life we were building, all the while feeling completely abandoned myself.

A few days after I broke up with him, I did what most women do—I got a new hairstyle. While in the chair at The Church of Hair, my good friend and intuitive hair designer, Terrell Anansi, helped me understand exactly why I ran when he said, "The people we're attracting have the same level of pain we have. The way we treat them is the way we treat ourselves." Ope! Until 2020, I didn't know how to stay with myself and not retreat or numb out of fear, and I certainly had no practice doing such a courageous thing in relationship with another. After the breakup, my body was grateful and my inner child was lost and in despair. It wasn't until weeks later that I made the connection that my body experienced so much pain because our relationship energy and the triggers we encountered activated the remaining stored trauma and childhood neglect I'd endured.

The power of healing and personal development work took me farther than I'd gone before—but not as far as I wanted. I fucked up. Breaking up in the way I did was a harrowing choice and I not-so-secretly prayed the separation would be temporary. At the same time, it was incredibly rewarding to follow-through on my own instincts, trusting that I'd be ok in the face of such a huge loss and blow to the heart. I definitely doubted myself and grieved. I also continued to move forward and focused on reinforcing my own connection to Source and maintaining my physical and mental health. I prayed a lot. I felt my feelings and shed tears instead of stuffing them down. I moved my body and I danced. I focused on my business and made new plans for my future. I was shaken for sure, but I wasn't knocked off center—primarily because I'd done so much healing work.

In every aspect of life, including business, love, wealth, and freedom, it's important to maintain focus and dedicate attention to the connection we have with ourselves and the Universal supports and synchronicities available. Every person possesses an inherent value that's completely independent of anything outside themselves. Regardless of what our current life circumstances reflect, the reality is that it's full of love, abundantly prosperous, and limitless. That's true for our personal life, spiritual connection, bank account balance, love life, business connections, and the freedom to live life on our own terms. Remaining present with our connection, focusing on the desired result, and taking inspired action is the fastest way to invite our dreams to appear—especially when things don't go as expected.

When things in my relationship didn't go as expected, I was tempted to fall back into the "here we go again," loop and get stuck there. Instead, I revisited the chapters of this book and the sheer goodness I'd manifested through my words, intentions, and actions. Much of life's success is dependent on the ability to be open, discover, grow, manifest, repeat, and scale what we've learned. There's no doubt that these recent challenges opened me, caused me to discover new parts of myself, grow from the learnings, and manifest new desires. The hard work is well underway. I hesitate to say it's "done," because there will always be more challenges. At the same time, I feel like the past 18 months enabled me to accomplish most of the necessary work and create a brand-new foundation. Now it's time to simply repeat, scale, and LIVE my manifestations.

That sounds easier said than done. But it doesn't have to be hard. Here are the principles outlined in this book that will lead the way:

- Live life as the best version of you and only put your whole heart into endeavors that enliven you.
- Embrace your idiosyncrasies to find perfect matches who appreciate every aspect of who you are.
- Use discernment, alignment, and an abundant mindset to initiate demand.

- Demonstrate magnetic desire with an attractive "No."
- Play the numbers game and understand alignment trumps everything.
- Own and integrate all aspects of yourself to serve from a place of wholeness.
- Understand the power of freedom and living your best life.
- Connect and heal through authenticity and vulnerability.
- Apply the power of courtship to go "all the way" and create "Fuck yes!" responses to every inquiry.
- Create effortless loyalty and connection through attraction.
- Evaluate and strip away everything that doesn't positively contribute to wholeness.
- Know that success is a process, fuck ups are integral, and resiliency is your greatest currency.
- Use data to find and exploit every sweet spot you can— especially the orgasmic ones.
- Recognize the power of love and collaboration while addressing the challenges of independence.
- Invite intimacy and sexual pleasure into your experience.
- Build your empire with people you love.
- Give exclusively from a place of inspiration and generosity.
- Enter the competition and use funnels to secure deep connection.
- Protect commitments with clear expectations and the Four Agreements.
- Reflect on challenging endings as new beginnings and celebrate graduations to every new level.
- Tap into the magic and synchronicity that's available when you trust the Universe to lead your dance with life.
- Acquire "automagic" luck through deliberate healing, effective choices, and abundant collaboration to cultivate resonant love.
- Stay present, honor, appreciate, and live the manifestations you achieved.

Experiencing freedom and living your Ultimate Vida is a constant research experiment. Here's to the journey of data collection, accurate measurements, data analysis, truthful exploration, and continual evolution. Plus, tons of orgasmic bliss!

Maintaining existing manifestations and creating new, grander ones, requires that we keep on living. Despite heartbreak, being open-hearted invites new life. Love and appreciation for every experience begets more moments to appreciate. As we grow and technology evolves, finding the orgasmic sweet spot between love, sex, and business is a moving target. The process is greatly enhanced when we stay true to who we are, believe wholeheartedly in our dreams, honor our desires, stay orgasmic, and continue to enhance even the sweetest sweet spot.

*"Believe you deserve it and
the Universe will deliver it."*
—UNKNOWN

# RESOURCES

# COURSES AND COMMUNITY SUPPORT

**Awaken Your Inner Author**, www.awakenyourinnerauthor.com

Download Melissa's Magic system to *finally* write the book that's trapped in your mind and heart.

As aspiring authors, we dream of our book creating a movement for the world and financial freedom for ourselves. But far too often, what happens instead is the soul-crushing experience of publishing your book only to have sales fall flat, momentum stunted, and your potentially life-changing book reaches precious few people. We are dedicated to making sure your story ends quite differently -- with you creating the impact and income that you desire from your book. That's where the publishing partnership with Ultimate Vida comes in. Grounded with decades of experience in online marketing and building sound business models around books, we help authors sidestep landmines and reach their goals by providing actionable data (like title and cover testing), a deep and intimate understanding of who your audience actually is (which is bound to surprise you), strategic advice on offerings beyond the book, and ongoing monthly income opportunities that far exceed book royalties. Reach out to melissa@uncorpedinfluence.com to discuss strategies to make a splash with your book and incorporate the Ultimate Vida community experience and course as a new revenue stream.

# Join the Ultimate Vida Freedom Circle

Your Secret Weapon To Kiss Your Job Goodbye in as Little as 77 Days, Build an Online Tribe, and Leave a Legacy

As an Ultimate Vida Freedom Circle Member, you can:

- Create a baseline of time and financial freedom while doing work you love
- Access proprietary data and strategies to blissfully nail the sweet spot of sex, love and business
- Get FREE access to our flagship Freedom Blueprint course, which sells on its own for $1,500
- Use your newfound freedom to focus on health, wellness, relationships, and purpose...the things that make life worth living
- Connect with the world's most epic tribe of freedom seekers to enrich your life, help you achieve your goals, and form lifelong friendships
- Earn supplemental income or even life-changing monthly money by referring others into the community

Enjoy the Community for FREE for 14 days!

www.ultimatevida.com/orgasmic

# PLAYLISTS

I literally have a playlist for everything and played on shuffle my tunes jump from Christian to gangsta rap with a side of Christmas hymns. Like entrepreneurs, the tunes are as diverse and varied as we are. Because music is integral to an orgasmic life, I've curated several playlists to soundtrack your journey to discovering the sweet spot of love, sex, and business by simply being you.

**The Orgasmic Entrepreneur**, bit.ly/OrgasmicEntrepreneurPlaylist
This playlist contains songs that are related to being one's true self—that includes being centered, connected, fun, and a bit rebellious.

**Ultimate Vida**, bit.ly/UltimateVidaPlaylist
This playlist contains songs that inspire you to live your best life—one that's free, connected, and prosperous.

**TranscenDANCE Manifesting Love**, bit.ly/ManifestingLovePlaylist
Love is exciting and fun. This playlist is full of lov songs to get you thinking about your "fuck yes and nothing less" love.

**TranscenDANCE Get it On**, bit.ly/GetItOnPlaylist
This playlist is filled with sexy (and explicit) songs to support orgasmic bliss.

Follow me on Spotify to access all of my playlists.

# REFERENCED BOOKS AND RECOMMENDED READING

OTHER BOOKS FROM THE AUTHORS:

**Melissa Drake**, *TranscenDANCE: Lessons from Living, Loving, and Dancing*

**Jesse Panama**, *The Art of Freedom: Kiss Your Job Goodbye, Build a Tribe, Leave a Legacy*

TEDx:

**The Dance of Collaboration**, bit.ly/MDrakeTEDx

REFERENCED BOOKS AND RECOMMENDED READING:

**Shawn Achor**, *The Happiness Advantage: The Seven Principles of Positive Psychology That Fuel Success and Performance at Work*

**Bob Burg and John David Mann**, *Go-Givers Sell More*

**Bob Burg and John David Mann**, *The Go-Giver*

**Kyle Cease**, *The Illusion of Money: Why Chasing Money Is Stopping You from Receiving It*

**Gary Chapman, PhD,** *The 5 Love Languages: The Secret to Love that Lasts*

**Gary Chapman, PhD and Paul White, PhD,** *The 5 Languages of Appreciation in the Workplace: Empowering Organizations by Encouraging People*
appreciationatwork.com

**Sonia Choquette**, *Ask Your Guides: Connecting to Your Divine Support System*

**Robert Holden, Ph.D.**, *Loveability: Knowing How to Love and Be Loved*

**Vishen Lakhiani**, *The Buddha and the Badass: The Secret Spiritual Art of Succeeding at Work*

**Dr. Nicole LePera,** *How to Do the Work: Recognize Your Patterns, Heal from Your Past, and Create Your Self*

**Zak Roedde**, *Irresistibly Feminine: How to Activate a Man's Everlasting Devotion to Your Heart*

**Don Miguel Ruiz**, *The Four Agreements: A Practical Guide to Personal Freedom (A Toltec Wisdom Book)*

**Bessel van der Kolk M.D.**, *The Body Keeps the Score: Brain, Mind, and Body in the Healing of Trauma*

**Pete Walker**, *Complex PTSD: From Surviving to Thriving*

# MELISSA DRAKE
## ABOUT THE AUTHOR

www.uncorpedinfluence.com

Melissa Drake is a woman continually evolving to live her Ultimate Vida—a life that's full of freedom, self-expression, work that makes a difference, cultural diversity, love, orgasmic bliss, wholeness, and rich rewards. Once confined to her bed from major depressive disorder and trapped in the corporate world, she worked her way up from an entry-level position to a director-level role reporting to the CEO. When middle-age life and an empty nest presented a wake-up call in the form of two concurrent chronic illnesses and a job loss after a 25-year career, she turned to social media and dancing for a reprieve.

Melissa's journey included extensive research in healing modalities, revolutionary personal transformation, a cross-country move from the Midwest to California, full-time entrepreneurship, a TEDx Talk, "The Dance of Collaboration," and her first book, TranscenDANCE: Letting the Universe Lead. An intuitive life coach and NLP practitioner with a BA in Business Management, Melissa has helped hundreds of coaches and healers to connect, collaborate, and heal through living their truth, seeking new adventures, writing their stories, and empowering others.

As the leader of Ultimate Vida LLC's publishing venture, Melissa is a compassionate coach and solutions-based resource who supports authors in publishing their books and exploring new income opportunities.

The Orgasmic Entrepreneur is Melissa's second book. She has published over 100 articles on such top-rated sites as Entrepreneur, Lifehack, Refinery29, The Mighty, Scary Mommy, The Good Men Project, Thrive Global, and Women for One. Melissa writes, edits, speaks, and leads workshops helping others expand and realize their dreams. Read more and connect with her at uncorpedinfluence.com.

# JESSE PANAMA
## FEATURED AUTHOR

www.ultimatevida.com

Jesse "retired" from the corporate world in 1998 at the ripe old age of 23 and became a pioneer of online marketing, then in its infancy. For the past 23 years, he's been an internet entrepreneur, running his businesses from every continent except Antarctica. The one thing Jesse always longed for was a step-by-step blueprint for how to leave your job, make money online while helping people, and live life on your own terms. He couldn't find one, so he wrote *The Art of Freedom* and is honored to be your freedom Sherpa welcoming you to the Ultimate Vida Community.

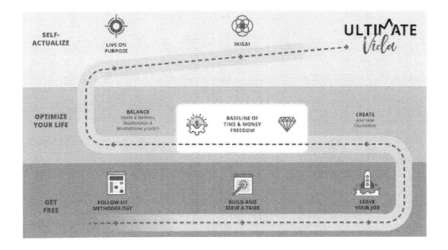

# JO DECHENNE
## FEATURED AUTHOR

www.thesacredsight.com

Jo DeChenne is a psychic intuitive, energetic healer who uses telekinesis and light language to move illness, depression, anxiety, and more out of the body. Here's a recap of her story:

I was born and raised in Northern California in the 1970s. I moved to Colorado at age 21 and settled in Denver. I have always been interested in all matters metaphysical and spiritual. I spent 20 years of my life working in accounting, a job that never interested me at all. It was only a means to an end. I was diagnosed with breast cancer in 2015, the same time I was dealing with a broken sacrum. Needless to say, I stopped working. I went through some pretty abject darkness.

In facing my own mortality, I magically rediscovered life. I realized I could never take "the little things" for granted again. I healed. In 2018, I started to pick up psychic information from everyone I met. In 2019, I took a trip to Disneyland with my husband and read the book "Ask Your Guides" by Sonia Choquette. Upon connecting with my first Guide, I knew life was never going to be the same.

My spirit guides immediately directed me to open a practice called The Sacred Sight, LLC. I followed their directions and my practice is thriving. I work with angels of all kinds. The archangels are my personal favorites. What those beings are capable of is incredible. On that Disney trip I realized I could move things with my mind and energy. When I work with people now, I move out toxic energies, trauma, false beliefs, psychic debris, low level entities, you name it. I am devoted to my work and I get to witness miracles on a daily basis. I'm a very lucky lady.

# STACEY HERRERA
## FEATURED AUTHOR

www.thesensualityproject.com

Stacey Herrera is an Intimacy & REALation-ship coach and writer. She is also the creator of The Sensuality Project, a lifestyle movement for 40+ singles and couples who want to improve their sex lives and have mature intimate relationships.

In Stacey's world, relationship-ing is about more than finding a right-fit partner and living happily ever after. Relationships inform the way we do business and how we treat our neighbors. It's about family—born and chosen. Because how you relate to the people around you can mean the difference between survival and fulfillment.

She believes that relationships are essential to our species' survival—like food, air, and water. This is why her mission is to help people get really good at relating to one another. It's not just about creating happiness in our personal lives—it's about creating peace and unity for the entire human race.

Stacey resides in a charming town on the coast of California. She spends her free time getting lost in books, baking cookies, and creating memories with her lovers, family, and friends.

www.cliffandmarta.com

Cliff and Marta Wilde are founders of The Unlimited Life and creators of the A.R.A. Method. Through nurturing AWARENESS, teaching radical RESPONSIBILITY and encouraging inspired ACTION – the A.R.A. method creates a powerful solution helping clients overcome dis-ease of both the physical body and the mind.

This dynamic team is often known as "The Health Fixers" because they create lasting results when everyone else failed. Using a holistic and multidisciplinary approach, Cliff and Marta do not tie into any one specific methodology. This flexibility allows them to treat everyone they work with a very personal and individualized approach, creating results that, to some, seem like magic.

So far, they've worked with hundreds of people from 25 countries. Clientele includes anyone from high-performing individuals like entre-preneurs and CEOs to world-class athletes, mums and dads, husbands and wives, no matter the social label.

Among other results, they've made several impossible pregnancies happen, co-created national champions, unraveled various mysterious and complex symptoms, helped end long-term depression, and put various "incurable" diseases into remission—including Cliff's ulcerative colitis (an autoimmune disease of the gut). He's now been medication- and symptom-free for 12 years.

Cliff and Marta are the people you call when you're ready to own your life, when you want to create emotional and physical health, and no one else can help.

# NOTES

## 1. AN EXCHANGE OF THE HEART

1. https://startupsusa.org/why-is-entrepreneurship-important/
2. https://s29814.pcdn.co/wp-content/uploads/2019/02/StateofIndependence-ResearchBrief-DigitalNomads.pdf
3. https://www.mbopartners.com/state-of-independence/2020-digital-nomads-report/

## 5. IT'S A NUMBERS GAME

1. https://www.prnewswire.com/news-releases/true-love-after-22-kisses-118160424.html

## 12. LOVE IS THE ANSWER

1. http://hr1973.org/docs/Harvard35thReunion_Waldinger.pdf
2. https://positivepsychologynews.com/news/george-vaillant/200907163163
3. https://papers.ssrn.com/sol3/papers.cfm?abstract_id=3470734
4. https://news.gallup.com/businessjournal/127043/friends-social-wellbeing.aspx

## 13. IT'S A PROCESS

1. https://www.forbes.com/profile/james-dyson/?sh=1d87bf8d2b38
2. https://www.wired.com/2011/04/in-praise-of-failure/
3. https://www.dyson.com/automotive

## 23. SELF-ACTUALIZATION AND SECURITY

1. https://www.novoed.com/wp-content/uploads/2019/01/NovoEd-Stanford-Study-Shows-Efficacy-of-Team-based-Online-Learning.pdf
2. https://jamesclear.com/how-can-i-be-happy-if-you-are-sad

Made in the USA
Middletown, DE
09 November 2021